GED
STUDY GUIDE

Reclaim Your Future and Expand Career Opportunities
Your Ultimate Guide with Proven Strategies and Practice Tests
to Ace All Four Parts of the GED Exam with Scores of 150+

SUCCESS ACADEMY PREP

TABLE OF CONTENTS

DISCLAIMER

The questions and reading passages presented in this book have been meticulously crafted by the author using a variety of online resources, including official practice tests. These materials have been adapted, modified, and created anew to suit the instructional purposes of this text.

It is important to note that while every effort has been made to ensure the quality and accuracy of the questions and passages, they are not endorsed by the GED Testing Service, the organization responsible for the GED exam. Additionally, the questions and passages in this masterclass may not be indicative of actual GED exam questions, and no guarantee is made regarding their resemblance to questions that may appear on the official exam.

Furthermore, any similarities between the questions and passages in this book and those found on official GED exams are purely coincidental. The primary goal of this text is to provide students with comprehensive practice and instruction to aid in their preparation for the GED exam.

By using this book, readers acknowledge and understand that the questions and passages are for educational purposes only and are not intended to replicate the exact content of the GED exam. The author and publisher assume no responsibility for any consequences resulting from the use or misuse of the materials presented herein.

HERE IS YOUR FREE GIFT!

REBUILD YOUR FUTURE: CONQUER THE GED WITH EXPERT STRATEGIES AND PRACTICE

Get your hands on our FREE BONUS. This essential pack is your golden ticket to shining in the GED exam, offering a full suite of tools that make learning a breeze. Boost your exam prep with online full-length practice tests and online videos. Unlock these free resources by scanning the QR code below.

Start your simplified journey to success in the GED today! Scan now and study confidently for the exam!

SCAN THE QR CODE TO DOWNLOAD THE GED BONUSES.

OR SIMPLY CLICK THE LINK https://qrco.de/bfP1Qg

How Can You Help with This book?

Creating this book at Excel Test Prep turned out to be quite challenging.

Understanding the topics is one thing, but laying them out logically, concisely, cohesively, and well-organized **to help you achieve the highest possible score on the exam** is a whole different ball game.

Additionally, we decided to avoid traditional publishing houses, opting instead for an independent publisher entirely focused on ensuring students' success, rather than serving other interests. This choice hasn't been without its struggles, but our dedication to helping others has won out.

That's why we'd be incredibly grateful if you could provide some feedback on Amazon. Your input would mean a lot to us and would greatly help us share this material with others. Here's what we recommend:

1. **If you haven't already, scan the QR code** at the start of the book and download the DIGITAL SAT BONUSES.

2. **Scan the QR code below or simply click the link and leave quick feedback on Amazon!**

CLICK THE LINK https://2ly.link/1zl0J

The best approach? Share a short video sharing your thoughts on the book! If that seems too much, no pressure at all. Feedback along with a couple of photos of the book would still be greatly appreciated!
Note: There's no obligation, but it would be immensely appreciated!
We are excited to embark on this journey with you. Ready to dive in?

Happy reading!

INTRODUCTION

The General Educational Development (GED) exam is a valuable opportunity for those who didn't complete high school but still want to achieve their educational and career goals. Whether you're looking to open doors to better job prospects, pursue higher education, or simply accomplish a personal milestone, the GED is your path forward.

The GED exam tests your knowledge in four key areas: Mathematical Reasoning, Reasoning Through Language Arts, Science, and Social Studies. It's designed to ensure you have the equivalent skills of a high school graduate, giving you a recognized credential that can help you move ahead in life.

The *GED Study Guide* will walk you through everything you need to know about the GED exam, providing tips, practice questions, and strategies to help you succeed. This book is an invitation to explore new perspectives, to challenge preconceptions, and to engage with ideas that resonate with the very core of our human experience.

The book is structured into nine pivotal parts, each designed to navigate the intricacies of the GED exam and empower you towards academic and professional success.

Part I: Understanding the GED Exam

The GED exam demonstrates your perseverance and dedication. It's a series of tests designed to measure your mastery of standard high school-level academic skills. Understanding the structure, content, and scoring of the GED is the first step in conquering it. This section explains the exam and helps you prepare.

Part II: Preparing for the Exam

In this section, we outline a study plan tailored to your unique needs, helping you balance your time between work, family, and study. We provide resources, study schedules, and techniques to optimize your learning experience.

Part III: Reasoning Through Language Arts

Language is the medium via which we communicate our ideas and thoughts. This section equips you with the tools to analyze texts, improve your writing skills, and effectively communicate your ideas, ensuring you're well-prepared for the language arts portion of the exam.

Part IV: Mathematical Reasoning

Mathematics is the language of logic. Our approach simplifies complex concepts into understandable lessons that build your confidence in tackling mathematical problems.

Part V: Science

Science is about understanding the world around us. This section provides a clear and concise review of fundamental scientific principles, preparing you to approach the science test with curiosity and confidence.

Part VI: Social Studies

Our society is full of historical events and civic principles. In this section, you'll explore key concepts in history, economics, geography, and civics, providing you with a solid foundation to answer social studies questions with ease.

Part VII: Tips and Tricks for the GED Exam

Every test has its strategies, and the GED is no exception. Here, we reveal exclusive tips and methods to help you handle the exam effectively. Learn how to approach different question types and manage your time effectively.

Part VIII: Practice Makes Perfect; The Full Exam Simulation

Practice is the essence of learning. This section contains a wealth of practice questions and exercises designed to hone your skills and build your test-taking stamina. It offers a full-length practice exam that mirrors the actual GED test, providing you with an opportunity to apply everything you've learned in a real-world setting.

As you start this educational adventure, remember that this guide is more than just pages filled with information—it's a key to a brighter future. Whether you're aiming to enhance your employment prospects, pursue higher education, or achieve a personal milestone, the *GED Study Guide* is here to support you every step of the way.

Let's learn together and achieve your academic goals.

PART I

UNDERSTANDING THE GED EXAM

OVERVIEW OF THE GED EXAM

The General Educational Development (GED) test is a comprehensive assessment that serves as a substitute for a high school diploma. It is designed to measure proficiency in standard high school subjects and is recognized in the United States and Canada as a key to opening doors to higher education and employment opportunities.

The GED exam helps people without a traditional high school education to showcase high school-level academic skills for external opportunities. It is a pathway to postsecondary education, workforce training programs, and better employment prospects. For many, the GED test represents a second chance at educational advancement and personal growth.

Regarding the Structure, the GED test is divided into four subject areas:

1. Mathematical Reasoning: This section tests arithmetic, algebra, geometry, and data analysis.

- Total Time: 115 minutes
- Total Number of Questions: Approximately 46

2. Reasoning Through Language Arts: This part assesses reading comprehension, writing, grammar, and the ability to analyze and construct arguments.

- Total Time: 150 minutes (including a 10-minute break)
- Total Number of Questions: Approximately 46

3. Science: The science test covers life sciences, physical science, earth and space science, and includes the application of scientific principles.

- Total Time: 90 minutes
- Total Number of Questions: Approximately 46

4. Social Studies: Covers history, economics, geography, and civics.

- Total Time: 70 minutes
- Total Number of Questions: Approximately 46

Adding these together, the GED exam typically has around 160-200 questions in total. This number can vary slightly due to the inclusion of different question types and experimental questions that do not count toward the final score.

Each subject test is scored on a scale of 100 to 200, with 145 being the minimum passing score for each. Scoring between 165-174 indicates college readiness, and a score of 175 or higher may qualify for college credits.

Preparation for the GED exam is critical for success. Examinees have access to numerous tools, including as official practice exams, study manuals, and online courses. Local adult education centers often offer GED preparation classes, providing personalized support and instruction.

Taking the Test and Post-Test Opportunities

Certified testing locations provide the GED test all year round. Candidates have the flexibility to take the tests one at a time and in any order. Depending on the subject, each session has a time limit that varies from 70 to 150 minutes.

Passing the GED test can significantly impact an individual's life. It is a stepping stone to higher education, where GED graduates can pursue college degrees or vocational training. A GED diploma can lead to improved job opportunities and higher pay. Additionally, it instills a sense of achievement and confidence in the graduates.

In a nutshell, the GED exam is more than just a test; it is a milestone for personal and professional development. It reflects a commitment to lifelong learning and the pursuit of one's goals. With the right preparation and determination, the GED test is a challenge that opens up a world of opportunities.

BENEFITS OF PASSING THE GED EXAM

Passing the General Educational Development (GED) exam has considerable benefits for people who have not completed a standard high school education. As a high school equivalency test, the GED exam provides an opportunity for individuals to demonstrate their knowledge and skills in key subject areas and earn a credential that is recognized by educational institutions, employers, and government agencies. In this comprehensive guide, we will explore the various benefits of passing the GED exam, ranging from expanded educational opportunities to improved career prospects and personal fulfillment.

1. Access to Higher Education

One of the most notable benefits of passing the GED exam is the opportunity to pursue higher education. Many colleges, universities, and vocational training programs recognize the GED as comparable to a high school diploma. With a GED diploma in hand, individuals can apply for admission to degree programs, technical schools, and certification courses, opening doors to a wide range of educational opportunities.

2. Expanded Career Opportunities

Passing the GED exam might open up new employment options and enhance earning potential. Many employers require a high school diploma or equivalent credential for entry-level positions. Obtaining a GED diploma, individuals demonstrate their commitment to education and their readiness for the workforce, making them more competitive candidates for employment.

3. Higher Earning Potential

Research has shown that individuals with a high school diploma or equivalent credential, such as a GED diploma, tend to earn higher wages than those without a diploma. Passing the GED exam can lead to increased earning potential over the course of a career, as it opens doors to higher-paying jobs and advancement opportunities in various industries.

4. Personal Fulfillment

For many individuals, obtaining a GED diploma is a source of personal fulfillment and pride. It represents overcoming challenges, acquiring new knowledge and skills, and achieving a significant milestone in one's education journey. Getting a GED can increase one's sense of self-worth and confidence, enabling them to pursue their ambitions with newfound vigor.

5. Setting a Positive Example

Passing the GED exam can serve as a positive example for family members, friends, and peers. It does so by demonstrating the importance of education and the value of perseverance, individuals who pass the GED exam inspire others to pursue their own educational and personal goals. They foster a culture of lifetime learning in their communities and serve as role models for the next generation.

6. Access to Military and Government Jobs

In addition to civilian employment opportunities, passing the GED exam can also open doors to careers in the military and government sectors. Many branches of the U.S. Armed Forces accept the GED credential for enlistment purposes, providing individuals with an alternative pathway to serve their country. Likewise, certain government agencies may require a high school diploma or equivalent credential for entry-level positions, making the GED diploma a valuable asset for aspiring civil servants.

7. Enhanced Job Stability and Security

Individuals who pass the GED exam are better positioned to secure stable and secure employment. With a high school equivalency credential, they are less likely to face unemployment or underemployment compared to those without a diploma. GED graduates have the knowledge and skills necessary to adapt to changing job market demands and pursue career paths that offer long-term stability and security.

8. Opportunity for Further Education and Training

Passing the GED exam is just the beginning of a lifetime of study and personal improvement. With a GED diploma in hand, individuals have the opportunity to pursue further education and training in their chosen field. Whether through college courses, vocational training programs, or professional development opportunities, GED graduates can continue to enhance their skills and knowledge to stay competitive in today's job market.

9. Improved Quality of Life

Those who earn a GED can benefit from higher living standards for themselves and their families. With access to higher education, expanded career opportunities, and increased earning potential, GED graduates can achieve financial stability and provide for their loved ones. Moreover, the sense of accomplishment and fulfillment that comes with passing the GED exam can positively impact overall well-being and happiness.

10. Breaking the Cycle of Poverty

Passing the GED exam is a major step in escaping poverty and ending the generational disadvantage loop for many people. Indeed, by obtaining a high school equivalency credential, individuals can overcome barriers to success and create a better future for themselves and their families. GED graduates become empowered to pursue their dreams and build a brighter tomorrow for future generations.

Generally, passing the GED exam offers a multitude of benefits, ranging from expanded educational opportunities to improved career prospects and personal fulfillment. Whether you want to further your education, advance your career, or simply fulfill a personal goal, obtaining a GED diploma opens doors to a brighter future. By earning this high school equivalency credential, you can demonstrate your determination, resilience, and readiness to succeed in today's competitive world.

HOW THE GED EXAM IS SCORED

The GED test assesses knowledge across four subject areas: Language Arts (Writing and Reading), Science, Social Studies, and Mathematics. Scoring on the GED exam is a crucial aspect that determines whether an individual achieves the necessary benchmark for high school equivalency. Here, we will go into the intricacies of how the GED exam is scored, examining the scoring methodology for each subject area and providing insights into the overall scoring process.

Overview of GED Scoring System

The GED exam scoring system aims to evaluate test-takers' proficiency in each subject area, providing a comprehensive assessment of their knowledge and skills. The scoring process involves various components, including multiple-choice questions, short answer responses, extended responses, and performance tasks. Each component contributes to the overall score in its respective subject area.

Subject Area Scoring:

1. Reasoning through Language Arts (Reading and Writing):

There are two components to the GED's RLA section: Reading and Writing. Both parts are scored separately, but the scores are combined to determine the overall performance in this subject area.

- **Reading Score:** The reading exam evaluates a candidate's comprehension of written passages and textual analysis skills. Test-takers encounter a variety of reading materials, such as drama, poetry, non-fiction, and fiction. The reading score is calculated using the number of right responses to multiple-choice questions.
- **Writing Score:** The Writing test assesses a candidate's ability to clearly and effectively articulate ideas in written English. It consists of both essay questions called the Extended Response and multiple-choice questions. The writing score is based on the correctness and coherence of responses to both types of questions.

2. Mathematics:

The mathematics section of the GED exam assesses mathematical reasoning and problem-solving skills. It covers a wide range of topics, including algebra, geometry, data analysis, and number operations.

- **Score Calculation:** The math test contains MCQs and problem-solving response blocks. The score is calculated based on the number of correct answers to multiple-choice questions and the accuracy of responses to constructed response items. The scoring rubric considers not only the final answer but also the process and logic used to arrive at it.

3. Science:

The Science exam assesses a candidate's comprehension of scientific ideas, theories, and procedures. It spans several scientific disciplines, such as environmental science, earth science, physics, chemistry, and biology.

- **Score Determination:** Similar to other subject areas, the Science test combines multiple-choice questions with short answer and extended response items. The score is determined based on the correctness and depth of understanding demonstrated in the responses.

4. Social Studies:

The Social Studies section evaluates knowledge of history, geography, civics, economics, and other social sciences.

- **Scoring Method:** Test-takers encounter multiple-choice questions as well as short answer and extended response items in this section. The scoring criteria emphasize the accuracy of responses and the ability to analyze historical events, interpret data, and understand social phenomena.

Scoring Criteria and Rubrics:

In addition to correct answers, the GED exam scoring rubrics consider various factors to evaluate the quality of responses. These factors may include:

- **Accuracy:** The correctness of answers is crucial, particularly in multiple-choice questions. However, in constructed response items, accuracy is assessed not only in the final answer but also in the process and reasoning demonstrated.
- **Clarity and Coherence:** In essay or extended response items, clarity of expression and coherence of ideas play a significant role. Test takers are evaluated on their ability to organize thoughts rationally, utilize suitable language, and maintain coherence throughout the response.
- **Depth of Understanding:** Scoring also considers the depth of understanding demonstrated in responses. Test-takers who can provide insightful analysis, make connections between different concepts, and demonstrate a nuanced understanding of the subject matter may receive higher scores.

Quantitative Breakdown of GED Scoring

To provide a clearer quantitative understanding of the GED exam scores, here are the specific scoring details for each section:

1. Reasoning Through Language Arts (RLA)

- **Total Score Range:** 100 - 200
- **Passing Score:** 145

- **College Ready Score:** 165 - 174
- **College Ready + Credit Score:** 175 - 200

2. Mathematical Reasoning

- **Total Score Range:** 100 - 200
- **Passing Score:** 145
- **College Ready Score:** 165 - 174
- **College Ready + Credit Score:** 175 - 200

3. Science

- **Total Score Range:** 100 - 200
- **Passing Score:** 145
- **College Ready Score:** 165 - 174
- **College Ready + Credit Score:** 175 - 200

4. Social Studies

- **Total Score Range:** 100 - 200
- **Passing Score:** 145
- **College Ready Score:** 165 - 174
- **College Ready + Credit Score:** 175 - 200

Total Score

- **Overall GED Exam Score Range:** 400 - 800 (sum of the four subject scores)
- **Overall Passing Score:** 580 (an average of 145 on each of the four tests)
- **College Ready Overall Score:** 660 - 700
- **College Ready + Credit Overall Score:** 700 – 800

Important Notes

- **Passing Criteria:** A minimum score of 145 in each subject is required to pass. Test-takers need to achieve a combined total score of at least 580 across all four subjects to earn the GED credential.
- **Scoring Levels:** Scores are divided into different levels to indicate high school equivalency (145 - 164), college readiness (165 - 174), and college readiness with potential college credits (175 - 200).

These specific numbers provide a clear, quantitative framework for understanding GED scores, helping test-takers to set goals and measure their progress accurately.

Overall Scoring Process:

Once the individual subject area scores are determined, they are combined to calculate the overall GED exam score. Normalization may be used in the scoring process to maintain consistency across multiple test forms and administrations. Essentially, normalization adjusts scores based on the relative difficulty of the test version taken by the candidate, ensuring fairness and validity of the scoring process.

Passing Score and High School Equivalency:

The passing score for the GED exam is set by each state or jurisdiction and may vary slightly depending on specific requirements. A passing score often means that the test-taker has proven to have the knowledge and abilities of a high school graduate. Those who successfully complete the GED exam are awarded a high school equivalency diploma, which is accepted as verification of academic ability by government organizations, employers, and educational institutions.

In summary, the scoring process of the GED exam is a comprehensive and rigorous assessment of test-takers' knowledge and skills across various subject areas. By evaluating responses to different types of questions, including multiple-choice, short answer, and extended response items, the scoring system provides a holistic measure of academic proficiency. Through careful consideration of scoring criteria and rubrics, the GED exam aims to ensure fairness, validity, and reliability in assessing high school equivalency. Ultimately, achieving a passing score on the GED exam opens doors to educational and employment opportunities, allowing individuals to pursue their academic and career goals.

REGISTERING FOR THE GED EXAM

For those who want to obtain a high school equivalency diploma, registering for the General Educational Development (GED) exam is an essential first step. The registration process involves several steps, including eligibility verification, selecting a test center, scheduling the exam, and payment of fees. In this comprehensive guide, we will explore each stage of the GED exam registration process in detail, providing valuable insights and tips for prospective test-takers.

Understanding GED Eligibility:

Knowing the requirements for qualifying as stated by the GED Testing Service is crucial before registering for the exam. In general, those who meet the following conditions are qualified to take the GED exam:

1. **Age Requirement:** The majority of states mandate that test takers be at least 16 years old. This may differ from state to state. Some states may also have additional restrictions for minors, such as parental consent.
2. **Education Status:** Test-takers must not be enrolled in high school and must not have graduated from high school or obtained a high school diploma or equivalent credential.
3. **Residency:** Normally, there are no residence requirements in place in order to take the GED exam. Anyone can sign up for the exam regardless of their state, place of work or country of residence.
4. **Additional Requirements:** Some states or jurisdictions may have additional eligibility criteria, such as minimum residency duration or completion of a GED preparation program. It's important to check the specific requirements of your state or jurisdiction before registering for the exam.

Regional Policy Variations

While the GED Testing Service provides general eligibility guidelines, specific registration requirements can vary significantly from state to state. For example, the general rule is that test-takers must be at least 16 years old, but some states may require additional documentation for those under 18, such as parental consent or proof of withdrawal from high school.

In terms of education status, some states may have unique criteria for individuals who were homeschooled or attended alternative education programs. Residency requirements can also differ; while generally, there are no residency restrictions, some states may require test-takers to have been residents for a certain period and provide proof of residency.

Additionally, some states may impose further requirements, such as the completion of a state-approved GED preparation course or passing a practice test before registering for the exam. States with age restrictions might also require younger test-takers to obtain a waiver by meeting specific conditions, such as being employed or enrolled in a job training program.

To find the specific eligibility requirements for your state, visit the official GED Testing Service website at GED.com.

Steps to Register for the GED Exam:

Once you have confirmed your eligibility to take the GED exam, you can proceed with the registration process. The steps involved in registering for the GED exam typically include the following:

1. Create an Account on the GED Website:

Account creation on the GED website is the first step. You can access the website once again GED.com. Creating an account allows you to access various resources, schedule your exam, and receive updates about the testing process.

2. Provide Personal Information:

During the account creation process, you will be asked to provide personal information, including your name, date of birth, contact information, and residency status. Since the information you submit will be used for registration and communication, it is crucial to make sure it is correct and current.

3. Verify Eligibility:

Before proceeding further, you may be required to verify your eligibility to take the GED exam. This may involve answering questions about your education status, age, and residency. Depending on your jurisdiction, additional documentation or proof of eligibility may be required.

4. Select Test Subjects:

Following verification of your eligibility, you will need to decide which test subjects to take. Language Arts (Reading and Writing), Science, Mathematics, and Social Studies are the four subject areas that make up the GED exam. Depending on your interests and readiness, you can register for any of the four disciplines separately or all four at once.

Note: It is necessary to take all four subjects to obtain the GED credential.

5. Choose a Test Center:

After selecting the test subjects, you will need to choose a test center where you will take the exam. Test centers are facilities equipped to administer the GED exam in a proctored environment. The GED website's test center finding function allows you to search for available test centers near your location.

6. Schedule Your Exam:

Once you have selected a test center, you can proceed to schedule your exam appointment. Test appointments are normally available at certain times and dates, although availability may change based on the schedule of the testing facility. To guarantee your desired day and time, it is best to plan your exam well in advance.

7. Review Exam Policies and Procedures:

Before taking the GED exam, you should review the GED Testing Service's exam policies and procedures. This includes information on exam day requirements, prohibited items, testing accommodations, and other relevant guidelines. Reviewing these policies will help ensure a smooth and successful testing experience.

To check the detailed exam policies and procedures for the GED, visit the official GED Testing Service website at GED.com. On the website, you can find comprehensive information in the "Policies" section.

8. Pay Exam Fees:

Paying the exam fees is the final step in the registration process. The cost of the GED exam varies significantly by state and can depend on whether you take the test online or at a test center. Here's a detailed breakdown of the costs:

1. Cost Per Subject:

- **In-Person Testing:** Fees generally range from $4 to $50 per subject. For example, in Arkansas, the in-person fee is as low as $4 per subject, while in South Dakota, it is $50 per subject.
- **Online Testing:** Fees typically range from $30 to $50 per subject. In most states, online testing is slightly more expensive than in-person testing. For instance, in California, the online test fee is $41 per subject, whereas the in-person fee is also $41 per subject.

2. Total Cost for All Subjects:

- The total cost for the complete GED exam (all four subjects) ranges from approximately $120 to $200, depending on the state. Some states offer free or reduced-cost testing. For example, Connecticut and New York provide free GED testing to eligible residents, while other states, like Texas, charge around $36.25 to $42.45 per subject.

3. Financial Aid and Fee Waivers:

- Certain states offer financial aid programs or fee waivers for individuals experiencing financial hardship. These programs can significantly reduce or eliminate the cost of taking the GED. For example, Connecticut offers free GED testing to applicants under the age of 21 and veterans, while other states may provide similar benefits to residents meeting specific criteria.

4. Discounts for Retakes:

- Many states offer reduced rates for retaking a failed test. The first two retakes of each subject are often provided at a discounted rate within a certain timeframe, usually within a year of the first attempt.

For the most accurate and up-to-date information regarding GED exam fees in your state, visit the official GED Testing Service website.

Tips for a Successful GED Exam Registration:

Registering for the GED exam can be a straightforward process if you follow these tips:

1. **Check Eligibility Requirements:** Before registering for the exam, carefully review the eligibility criteria set forth by the GED Testing Service and your state or jurisdiction. Check all requirements before continuing with registration.

2. **Plan Ahead:** This helps you book your preferred date, time, and test center. Avoid registering at the last minute because space may be restricted, particularly during the busiest times for testing.

3. **Gather Required Information:** Obtain all required information, including contact data, educational background, and personal details, before beginning the registration process. This will streamline everything.

4. **Review Test Subject Requirements:** Familiarize yourself with the content and format of the GED exam's subject areas. Assess your strengths and weaknesses in each subject and select the test subjects that align with your skills and knowledge.

5. **Understand Exam Policies:** Spend some time reading through and comprehending the GED Testing Service's exam policies and procedures. Familiarize yourself with exam day requirements, prohibited items, and other important guidelines to ensure compliance.

6. **Prepare for the Exam:** While registration is the first step, adequate preparation is essential for success on the GED exam. Enrol in a GED preparation program, use study materials and resources, and practice with sample questions to increase your readiness.

7. **Stay Informed:** Keep yourself updated on any changes to the GED exam registration process, test policies, or processes. Regularly check the official GED Testing Service website for announcements and updates.

Essentially, you must remember to check eligibility requirements, select test subjects, choose a test center, schedule your exam, review exam policies, and pay exam fees in a timely manner. With proper planning and preparation, you can take the first step toward reaching your academic and professional goals with the GED exam.

PART II
PREPARING FOR THE EXAM

SETTING UP YOUR STUDY PLAN

A study plan is a strategic approach to preparing for the GED exam. It is the blueprint that guides your study efforts and ensures that you cover important topics efficiently and effectively. A well-crafted study plan takes into account your current knowledge, learning style, and the time you have available, allowing you to maximize your study sessions and retain more information.

Creating a study plan is akin to mapping out a journey; it provides direction and keeps you focused on the destination. Without a plan, it's easy to become overwhelmed by the volume of material or to neglect areas that require additional attention. A study plan also helps in tracking progress, managing time, and staying motivated throughout the preparation process.

Assessing Your Knowledge

Making a study plan starts with determining your present level of expertise. This is crucial in identifying which areas you are already proficient in and which areas require more focus. By taking practice tests for each subject, you can gauge your understanding and tailor your study plan to address your specific needs.

This initial assessment provides a foundation upon which to build new knowledge. It also boosts confidence, as you can see the progress you're making as you study.

Setting Goals

Goal setting is a powerful tool in any endeavor, and preparing for the GED exam is no exception. Be realistic and specific. Think about the exam date you want to take the test and the scores you hope to obtain. These goals should serve as motivation, pushing you to study consistently and effectively.

Break down your goals into scalable tasks. For instance, you might set a goal to master a particular math concept or to improve your reading comprehension by a certain degree before moving onto the advance step. These smaller goals help to create a sense of achievement as you progress, keeping you engaged and committed to your study plan.

Creating a Study Schedule

Your study schedule is the cornerstone of your GED preparation. It ought to represent the amount of time you can actually commit to learning each subject. Consistency is key; establish a set daily routine. This facilitates habit formation and makes following your plan easier.

When creating your schedule, consider other commitments and plan your study times around them. Studying early in the day may be more beneficial if you're a morning person. On the other hand, plan your study sessions for the evenings if that's when you're most alert. The important thing is to find a rhythm that works for you and to adhere to it as closely as possible.

Selecting Study Materials

The materials you choose for your GED study are just as important as the time you put in. There are numerous tools accessible, including online classes, practice exams, and official GED study manuals. It's essential to select materials that are up-to-date and that resonate with your learning style.

Consider a mix of different types of materials. For example, you might use books for in-depth study, online resources for interactive learning, and practice tests to gauge your understanding. Diversifying your study materials can keep you engaged and can cater to different aspects of learning, such as visual, auditory, and kinesthetic.

Study Techniques

Effective study techniques can enhance your learning and retention. Active reading, which involves critically asking questions about passages and deducting what comes next, is helpful. Taking notes is another useful strategy that facilitates knowledge organization and facilitates later evaluation.

Experiment and see what clicks. Some people find it helpful to teach the material to someone else, as it requires a deep understanding of the topic. Others use mnemonic devices to memorize facts and concepts. The secret is to be proactive in how you undertake your studies, rather than passively reading or listening to information. You can find further learning on this topic in the next section "Study Techniques for Success."

Practice Tests

Practice tests are a critical component of your GED study plan. They provide a benchmark for your current knowledge and help you get an idea of the format and timing of the real exam. Taking practice tests under exam conditions can also reduce anxiety on test day, as you'll know what to expect.

Review your answers at the end, including the correct and incorrect among what you couldn't answer. This review process is where much of the learning happens. It allows you to identify patterns in your mistakes and to focus your study efforts on areas that need improvement. Practice questions can be found in Part VII.

Seeking Support

Studying for the GED exam doesn't have to be a lonely endeavor. Seeking support from study groups, educators, or tutors can provide motivation and accountability. It can also offer different perspectives on the material and can help clarify concepts that you might find challenging.

Feel free to reach out for help when you need it. Whether it's joining a study group or hiring a tutor, having support can make a significant difference in your preparation. It can also make the study process more enjoyable and less daunting.

Health and Wellness

Your physical and mental health is important if you want to study effectively. A balanced diet, exercising regularly, and having adequate sleep daily can improve concentration, memory, and overall cognitive function. It's good to take proper care of your body to support your mind.

Take brief mental pauses in-between sessions. Short breaks are helpful in preventing fatigue and you will feel rejuvenated and attentive. It's also important to manage stress using techniques or hobbies that you enjoy. A healthy balance between studying and leisure can lead to better outcomes.

Review and Adjust

As you progress in your GED preparation, it's important to regularly review and adjust your study plan. This might mean spending more time on a challenging subject or adjusting your goals as you improve. Being flexible and responsive to your needs is key to an effective study plan.

Reviewing your plan also allows you to celebrate your successes. Acknowledging progress can be a great motivator. Don't be too hard on yourself if you need to make changes; the goal is to create a plan that works for you.

Time Management

Time management is an essential skill for GED preparation. By managing your time well, you can ensure that you cover important material without feeling overburdened.

Use calendars, planners, or apps to manage your study schedule and deadlines. Be realistic about how much you can achieve in each study session and set specific goals for what you want to accomplish. This will help you make the most of your sessions or study time.

Stress Management

Preparing for the GED exam can be stressful, but there are ways to manage this stress. Mindfulness techniques can help calm your mind and reduce anxiety. Find ways of managing stress or strategies that work for you.

Remember that it's fine to take breaks and to step away from studying when you need to. Taking care of your mental health is equally as crucial as covering the material. Find activities that relax you and make time for them in your routine.

Utilizing Technology

Technology can be of great help in your GED preparation. There are many educational apps and online courses available that can provide interactive and engaging ways to learn. These tools can offer a different approach to studying and can complement traditional study materials.

Consider using apps for flashcards, practice questions, or video tutorials. Online platforms and study groups can also be a great resource for support and information. Embrace technology as a part of your study plan, but be mindful of the potential for distraction.

Final Preparations

In the final weeks leading up to the GED exam, your focus should shift to reviewing and reinforcing your knowledge. Avoid trying to learn new stuff at this stage; instead, focus on areas where you still feel uncertain. This is the time to solidify what you've learned and to build confidence.

Take full-length practice tests to simulate the actual GED exam experience. Pay attention to your timing and work on any issues with pacing. The goal is to enter the exam room feeling prepared and calm, knowing that you've done everything you can to get ready.

Registration Process

Understanding the registration process for the GED exam is an important part of your preparation. Make sure you're familiar with the details, fees, and testing center locations. Check the official GED website for the most up-to-date information and check if you meet all the requirements.

Registering for the exam should be straightforward, but don't leave it until the last minute. Give yourself plenty of time to complete the process and to resolve any issues that might arise. Being proactive about registration can reduce stress and allow you to focus on your studies.

A comprehensive study plan is your roadmap to success on the GED exam. It should be tailored to your individual needs and learning style, and it should be flexible enough to adapt as you progress.

STUDY TECHNIQUES FOR SUCCESS

1. **Active Reading** Active reading involves engaging deeply with the text by questioning, predicting, and summarizing as you go. When you actively read, you should ask questions about the material to clarify your understanding, predict what might come next based on the context, and summarize key points in your own words. This technique helps improve comprehension and retention, making your study sessions more effective.

2. **Note-Taking** Note-taking is an essential skill for organizing and recording important information. Utilize methods like the Cornell Note-Taking System or outline method to highlight key concepts and details. Writing notes in your own words helps reinforce learning and makes review easier later on. It's important to regularly revisit and revise your notes to keep the information fresh in your mind.

3. **Mnemonic Devices** Mnemonic devices are memory aids that help you recall information more easily. Create acronyms, rhymes, or visual images that link new information with something familiar. For example, using "PEMDAS" (Parentheses, Exponents, Multiplication and Division, Addition and Subtraction) helps remember the order of operations in math. These devices can make complex information more manageable and memorable.

4. **Practice Testing** Practice testing involves taking practice exams to simulate the test environment and gauge your understanding. Use GED practice tests available online or in study guides, timing yourself to replicate real exam conditions. After completing a practice test, review your answers thoroughly to identify areas for improvement and understand why certain answers were incorrect.

5. **Teaching the Material** Teaching the material to someone else reinforces your own understanding. Explain concepts to a study partner or even to yourself out loud. This method requires you to process the information deeply, helping you to identify gaps in your knowledge and solidify what you've learned. Teaching can also boost your confidence in the subject matter.

6. **Mind Mapping** Mind mapping is a visual technique that helps you see the relationships between concepts. Create a diagram that connects ideas around a central concept, using branches to represent subtopics and link related ideas. This technique is particularly useful for subjects that involve complex interrelationships, such as history or science.

7. **Flashcards** Flashcards are a simple yet effective tool for memorizing key facts and concepts. Write questions on one side of a card and answers on the other. Review them regularly, shuffling often to ensure you're not just memorizing the order of the cards. Flashcards are especially useful for subjects that require a lot of memorization, like vocabulary or historical dates.

8. **Summarization** Summarization involves condensing information into brief summaries to capture the main points. After reading a section, write a summary in your own words, focusing

on the most important details. This technique helps reinforce your understanding and makes it easier to review large amounts of information quickly.

9. **Self-Explanation** Self-explanation requires you to explain the material to yourself as you study. After reading a passage or solving a problem, articulate the reasoning behind it out loud. This process helps deepen your understanding and can highlight any areas where you need further clarification.

10. **Spaced Repetition** Spaced repetition is a technique where you review information at increasing intervals. Use tools like Anki or Quizlet to schedule reviews of flashcards over days, weeks, or months. This method helps move information from short-term to long-term memory, making it a powerful tool for retaining knowledge over time.

11. **Group Study** Group study allows you to gain different perspectives and support from peers. Form a study group and meet regularly to discuss material, quiz each other, and share study tips. Studying with others can make the process more engaging and help clarify concepts that you might find challenging on your own.

12. **Use of Educational Apps** Leveraging technology can enhance your study experience. Use educational apps like Khan Academy, Coursera, or GED-specific apps for interactive lessons, videos, and practice questions. These tools offer a variety of learning formats, which can cater to different learning styles and make studying more dynamic.

13. **Visualization Techniques** Visualization involves creating mental images to understand and remember information. For example, you can visualize historical events, scientific processes, or mathematical concepts. This technique is particularly helpful for subjects that involve complex sequences or processes, as it allows you to see the information in a different way.

14. **Audio Learning (Podcasts, Lectures)** Audio learning can be a great supplement to traditional studying. Listen to educational podcasts or recorded lectures on GED subjects. This method is convenient for learning on the go and can be especially helpful for auditory learners who retain information better through listening.

15. **Interactive Learning Tools** Interactive learning tools engage you in active participation. Use online platforms that offer exercises, quizzes, and videos to reinforce learning. Interactive tools can make studying more enjoyable and help you retain information more effectively through active engagement.

16. **Time Blocking** Time blocking involves allocating specific times for studying different subjects. Divide your day into blocks of time dedicated to specific tasks or subjects. This method helps ensure you cover all necessary material and maintain a balanced study routine. Consistency is key, so stick to your schedule as closely as possible.

17. **Pomodoro Technique** The Pomodoro Technique helps maintain focus and prevent burnout. Study for 25 minutes, then take a 5-minute break. After four cycles, take a longer break. This technique helps keep your mind fresh and improves concentration during study sessions.

18. **Mock Exams** Taking mock exams simulates the actual exam experience. Set aside a day to take a full-length practice exam under timed conditions. This practice helps build stamina and familiarity with the test format, reducing anxiety on exam day. Review your performance afterward to identify areas for improvement.

19. **Goal Setting** Setting clear, achievable goals helps keep you motivated and on track. Define specific, measurable, attainable, relevant, and time-bound (SMART) goals for your study sessions. Breaking down your goals into smaller tasks can create a sense of achievement as you progress, keeping you engaged and committed.

20. **Frequent Review Sessions** Regular review sessions reinforce learning and help retain information. Schedule frequent reviews into your study plan to revisit notes, flashcards, and practice tests. Consistent review ensures that material stays fresh in your mind and helps identify areas that need further study.

MANAGING STUDY TIME AND RESPONSIBILITIES

Balancing study time with other responsibilities can be challenging, especially for those juggling work, family, or other commitments. Effective time management is crucial for success, not just in preparing for exams like the GED, but also in maintaining a healthy work-life balance. Here's how you can master this essential skill:

- Start by identifying your priorities. Determine what tasks are most important and urgent, and focus on those first. Setting clear, achievable goals is key. Break down your study objectives into specific tasks and set deadlines for each. This approach, known as goal-setting, helps keep you focused and motivated. For example, instead of a vague goal like "study math," set a specific target such as "complete three algebra practice problems by Friday."

- A well-organized study schedule is your roadmap to success. Begin by listing all your responsibilities, including work, family obligations, and leisure activities. Then, allocate specific time blocks for studying. Consistency is crucial; try to study at the same times each day to build a routine. Use tools like calendars, planners, or digital apps to keep track of your schedule. Be realistic about the time you can dedicate to studying each day, and ensure you have a balance between study and rest.

- Time-blocking is an effective strategy where you dedicate fixed time periods to specific tasks. For instance, you might block off 9 AM to 11 AM for GED preparation, followed by a break, and then work or other activities. This technique helps prevent multitasking and ensures that you give your full attention to one task at a time, which can significantly improve productivity.

- The Pomodoro Technique is a time management method that can enhance concentration and productivity. It involves working for 25 minutes, followed by a 5-minute break. After four cycles, take a longer break of 15-30 minutes. This method helps maintain focus and prevents burnout by ensuring regular intervals of rest.

- Life can be unpredictable, and sometimes your plans might not go as expected. It's important to be flexible with your schedule. If something urgent comes up, adjust your study plan accordingly. Regularly review and update your schedule to reflect any changes in your responsibilities or goals.

- Use technology to your advantage. There are numerous apps designed to help with time management and study planning. Apps like Trello, Asana, and Google Calendar can help you organize tasks and keep track of deadlines. Additionally, educational apps like Khan Academy and Quizlet offer resources that can make studying more efficient and effective.

- If you have other responsibilities, such as household chores or work tasks, consider delegating some of them. Sharing responsibilities with family members or colleagues can free up more time for studying. This can be especially helpful for parents or working adults who have multiple obligations.

- Effective time management isn't just about maximizing study time; it's also about maintaining a healthy balance. Ensure you get adequate sleep, eat healthily, and exercise regularly. Taking care of your physical and mental health is essential for optimal performance. Schedule regular breaks and leisure activities to recharge and prevent burnout.

- Keeping your study materials and workspace organized can save time and reduce stress. Have all your books, notes, and supplies in one place, and keep your study area clean and free from distractions. An organized environment can improve focus and make your study sessions more productive.

- Don't hesitate to seek support from friends, family, or study groups. Sharing your goals and progress with others can provide motivation and accountability. Study groups can also offer different perspectives and help clarify difficult concepts. Additionally, consider reaching out to tutors or educators if you need extra help with specific subjects.

Time management is a skill that requires practice and adjustment, but with persistence and the right approach, you can achieve your academic and personal goals.

OVERCOMING TEST ANXIETY

Overcoming test anxiety is a common challenge for many students, especially when facing a comprehensive exam like the GED.

Here's an extensive guide to help you manage and reduce test anxiety:

Understanding Test Anxiety

Test anxiety is a psychological condition where individuals experience extreme stress, anxiety, and discomfort during testing situations. This can impair their ability to perform to their potential. For GED candidates, who often face high stakes in obtaining their certification, test anxiety can be particularly daunting.

To manage it, we must recognize it. Physical symptoms may include sweating, shaking, rapid heartbeat, dry mouth, or nausea. Mental and emotional symptoms can range from feelings of dread and panic to negative self-talk, difficulty concentrating, and blanking out during the test.

Causes of Test Anxiety

The causes of test anxiety are multifaceted and can include fear of failure, lack of preparation, and negative past experiences. For GED students, the pressure to succeed and the weight of the exam's importance in their educational and career advancement can amplify these feelings.

Another contributing factor can be high personal expectations or external pressure from family and friends. Perfectionism and a tendency to equate self-worth with performance can also lead to heightened anxiety. Understanding these triggers is crucial in developing strategies to overcome test anxiety.

Preparing for the GED Exam

Preparation is key in reducing test anxiety. A well-structured study plan that covers all the GED subjects can build confidence and familiarity with the material. Utilize test-prep books and engage in multiple practice tests to become accustomed to the format and timing of the exam.

In addition to studying the content, it's important to familiarize yourself with the test-taking process. This includes understanding the rules and format of the GED exam, knowing what to expect on test day, and having a strategy for how to approach different types of questions. Being well-prepared can alleviate much of the anxiety associated with uncertainty.

Strategies to Manage Anxiety

Developing effective coping strategies is essential for managing test anxiety. Deep breathing and meditation are known to effectively mitigate anxiety. Engage in these whenever you find your state of mind disturbed.

Another tactic is to keep an optimistic outlook. Replace negative thoughts with affirmations and remind yourself of your preparation and past successes. It's also helpful to establish a support system of friends, family, or fellow students who understand what you're going through and can provide encouragement.

The Role of Sleep and Nutrition

Getting enough sleep and eating a healthy diet are important for controlling anxiety. Make sure you get enough sleep the night before both the exam and your study sessions. A well-rested mind can concentrate and remember knowledge better.

Similarly, eating a balanced diet can affect your energy levels and concentration. Over-the-top caffeine and sugar can worsen anxiety. Choose meals and snacks that stabilize blood sugar levels and offer long-lasting energy instead.

Test-Taking Techniques

On the day of the exam, use specialized test-taking tactics to assist control nervousness. To gain confidence, begin by answering questions you are familiar with before on to more difficult ones.

It's also critical to pace yourself. Keep an eye on the time, but do not rush. If you become stuck on a question, mark it and proceed; you may always come back to it later. This prevents you from spending too much time on one problem and running out of time for others.

After the Exam

Once the exam is over, it's important to reflect on the experience. Consider what strategies worked well for you and what you might do differently next time. This reflection can help you continue to improve your test-taking skills and reduce anxiety in future exams.

Additionally, engage in a relaxing activity after the exam to decompress. Whether it's spending time with friends, going for a walk, or watching a movie, taking time to unwind can help you mentally recover from the stress of the exam.

GED candidates can significantly reduce test anxiety and improve their performance on the exam by understanding and implementing these strategies. Remember, overcoming test anxiety is a process, and with the right tools and mindset, it is an achievable goal.

PART III
REASONING THROUGH LANGUAGE ARTS

anguage arts proficiency is a crucial component of the General Educational Development (GED) exam. This section assesses a test-taker's ability to comprehend written text, apply language conventions, and effectively communicate ideas through writing. In Part III of *The GED Study Guide*, we will comb through Reasoning Through Language Arts, focusing on two key areas: Reading for Meaning and Mastering Language Conventions and Usage.

READING FOR MEANING

Reading comprehension is a fundamental skill tested in the GED Reasoning Through Language Arts (RLA) section. Test-takers encounter various types of written passages, including fiction, non-fiction, poetry, and drama. The ability to understand and analyze these texts is essential for success on the exam. Here's how you can improve your reading comprehension skills:

Active Reading Strategies:

To enhance your comprehension, practice the following active reading strategies:

- **Previewing:** Before diving into the passage, take a moment to scan through it. Look at the title, headings, and images (if applicable). This will provide you with an overview and context before you start reading.
- **Annotating:** As you read, interact with the text by underlining or highlighting key information, unfamiliar words, and important details. Write brief summaries or questions in the margins to aid comprehension and retention.
- **Summarizing:** After completing each section or paragraph, pause to summarize the main idea in your own words. This helps reinforce your understanding and keeps you actively engaged with the text.

Analyzing Text Structure:

Understanding the structure of a passage can aid comprehension by revealing how information is organized and connected. Pay attention to:

- **Main Idea and Supporting Details:** Identify the central theme or argument of the passage, as well as the evidence or examples used to support it. Look for key phrases that indicate the main idea, such as thesis statements or topic sentences.
- **Chronological Order:** Notice the sequence of events or ideas presented in the text, especially in historical or narrative passages. Pay attention to transitional words and phrases that indicate changes in time or sequence.
- **Compare and Contrast:** Look for similarities and differences between ideas, characters, or events, as well as any cause-and-effect relationships. Pay attention to words like "however," "in contrast," and "similarly" that signal comparisons or contrasts.

Making Inferences and Drawing Conclusions:

In addition to understanding explicit information, the GED exam often requires test-takers to make inferences and draw conclusions based on implicit clues within the text. Practice these skills by:

- **Identifying Implicit Meanings:** Pay attention to tone, mood, and word choice to infer the author's attitude or purpose. Look for descriptive language or figurative language that conveys deeper meanings.
- **Drawing Logical Conclusions:** Use evidence from the text to make logical deductions about characters' motives, outcomes of events, or implications of ideas. Look for cause-and-effect relationships or patterns of behavior that suggest certain outcomes.
- **Predicting Outcomes:** Anticipate what might happen next in a story or how a situation might develop based on the information provided. Consider the characters' motivations, the context of the situation, and any foreshadowing clues.

Sample Passage and Analysis

Title: The Rise of Renewable Energy

In recent years, renewable energy sources such as wind, solar, and hydroelectric power have become increasingly popular. These energy sources are seen as essential in the fight against climate change because they produce little to no greenhouse gases. Additionally, advancements in technology have made renewable energy more affordable and efficient, allowing for broader adoption. Despite these benefits, the transition from fossil fuels to renewable energy has faced several challenges, including political opposition, high initial costs, and the need for significant infrastructure changes.

Governments worldwide are implementing policies to encourage the use of renewable energy. For example, tax incentives and subsidies help lower the financial barriers for both consumers and companies. Moreover, public awareness campaigns highlight the environmental and economic advantages of switching to renewables. As a result, more people are investing in renewable energy solutions, from solar panels on rooftops to electric vehicles.

As renewable energy technology continues to evolve, its role in the global energy market will likely expand. Researchers are developing more efficient solar cells, better battery storage systems, and more resilient wind turbines. These innovations promise to make renewable energy even more competitive with traditional fossil fuels. However, for a successful transition, it is crucial to address the current barriers and ensure that renewable energy infrastructure is robust and reliable.

Analysis of the Passage

Active Reading Strategies:

- **Previewing:** Before reading, glance at the title "The Rise of Renewable Energy." This title indicates that the passage will discuss the growing popularity and importance of renewable energy sources.
- **Annotating:** While reading, underline key information like "renewable energy sources such as wind, solar, and hydroelectric power" and "produce little to no greenhouse gases." Highlight phrases such as "advancements in technology" and "political opposition" to note significant details. Write in the margins next to these highlights to summarize points or ask questions, like "What are the specific advancements in technology?" and "How do subsidies lower financial barriers?"
- **Summarizing:** After reading the first paragraph, summarize it as follows: "Renewable energy is crucial for combating climate change but faces challenges like political opposition and high costs."

Analyzing Text Structure:

- **Main Idea and Supporting Details:** The central theme of the passage is the increasing importance and adoption of renewable energy. Supporting details include the benefits of renewable energy (produces little to no greenhouse gases, technological advancements) and the challenges (political opposition, high initial costs, infrastructure changes).
- **Chronological Order:** The passage does not follow a strict chronological order but does present a logical flow of ideas, from the current popularity of renewable energy to the challenges and future outlook.
- **Compare and Contrast:** The passage contrasts renewable energy with fossil fuels, noting the environmental benefits of renewables ("little to no greenhouse gases") versus the traditional reliance on fossil fuels. It also compares the current state of renewable energy technology with its potential future advancements.

Making Inferences and Drawing Conclusions:

- **Identifying Implicit Meanings:** By noting the tone and word choice, we can infer that the author is optimistic about the future of renewable energy. Phrases like "advancements in technology" and "promising innovations" suggest a positive outlook.
- **Drawing Logical Conclusions:** Based on the evidence provided, we can deduce that addressing the challenges (political opposition, costs, infrastructure) is crucial for the widespread adoption of renewable energy.

- **Predicting Outcomes:** Given the current trends and advancements, it is reasonable to predict that renewable energy will become more prevalent and competitive with fossil fuels in the near future.

MASTERING LANGUAGE CONVENTIONS AND USAGE

Mastering language conventions and usage is a critical aspect of the General Educational Development (GED) exam, particularly in the Reasoning Through Language Arts (RLA) section. This section evaluates a test-taker's ability to apply standard English grammar, punctuation, capitalization, and sentence structure rules to effectively communicate ideas in writing. In this comprehensive guide, we will explore the art of mastering language conventions and usage for the GED exam, covering grammar rules, punctuation guidelines, capitalization principles, and strategies for constructing clear and coherent sentences.

Grammar Rules: Achieving success on the GED exam requires a strong grasp of grammar principles. Test-takers must demonstrate proficiency in identifying and applying various grammatical concepts, including:

1. Parts of Speech:

Key parts of speech include:

Nouns: Words that represent people, places, things, or ideas.

- *Examples:* teacher, city, book, freedom.

Pronouns: Terms used in place of nouns to prevent repetition.

- *Examples:* he, she, it, they.

Verbs: Words that convey an action, feeling, or condition.

- *Examples:* run, think, is, become.

Adjectives: Words that alter or characterize nouns.

- *Examples:* happy, blue, large, quick.

Adverbs: Words that modify verbs, adjectives, or other adverbs.

- *Examples:* quickly, very, well, silently.

Prepositions: Words that indicate how pronouns or nouns relate to other words in a phrase.

- *Examples:* in, on, at, between.

Conjunctions: Words that join phrases, sentences, or clauses.

- *Examples:* and, but, or, because.

Interjections: Words that convey surprise or feeling.

- *Examples:* wow, ouch, hey, oh.

2. Sentence Structure:

Understanding sentence structure allows test-takers to construct clear and coherent sentences. Key concepts include:

Subject-Verb Agreement

Ensuring that the subject and verb of a sentence agree in number (singular or plural) is fundamental. A mismatch can make a sentence confusing and grammatically incorrect.

Examples:

- **Singular:** *The cat (singular subject) runs (singular verb) across the yard.*
- **Plural:** *The cats (plural subject) run (plural verb) across the yard.*
- **Compound Subject:** *The dog and the cat (compound subject) play (plural verb) together.*

Verb Tense Consistency

Maintaining consistent verb tense throughout a sentence or paragraph helps to clearly indicate the timing of actions. Shifting tenses can confuse the reader and disrupt the flow of your writing.

Examples:

- **Consistent Past Tense:** *She danced gracefully and then sat down.*
- **Consistent Present Tense:** *He is reading a book and sipping tea.*
- **Inconsistent Tense:** *She dances gracefully and then sat down.* (should be "dances" and "sits" or "danced" and "sat")

Parallelism

Parallelism involves using the same grammatical structure for similar elements within a sentence. This technique improves readability and creates a pleasing rhythm.

Examples:

- **Parallel:** *She likes hiking, swimming, and biking.*
- **Not Parallel:** *He enjoys reading books, to write essays, and drawing.* (should be "reading books, writing essays, and drawing")
- **Parallel Comparisons:** *She is not only intelligent but also creative.*

Clauses and Phrases

Understanding the difference between independent clauses (complete sentences) and dependent clauses (incomplete sentences) is crucial for forming complex sentences. Independent clauses can stand alone, while dependent clauses need an independent clause to form a complete thought.

Examples:

- **Independent Clause:** *She went to the store.* (a complete sentence)
- **Dependent Clause:** *Because she needed milk.* (incomplete sentence)
- **Complex Sentence:** *She went to the store because she needed milk.* (combines both clauses)
- **Phrase Example:** *Running through the park,* she felt invigorated. (the phrase "running through the park" adds information but is not a complete sentence on its own)

3. Usage:

Applying correct grammar usage involves understanding when and how to use specific words and phrases in context. Common usage errors to avoid include:

Misplaced and Dangling Modifiers

Modifiers are words or phrases that provide additional information about another element in the sentence. Misplaced or dangling modifiers can lead to confusion or ambiguity.

Misplaced Modifier Example:

- **Incorrect:** *She almost drove her kids to school every day.* (Suggests she almost did it but didn't)
- **Correct:** *She drove her kids to school almost every day.* (Clarifies that she frequently drove them)

Dangling Modifier Example:

- **Incorrect:** *Running quickly, the finish line seemed far away.* (Who was running?)
- **Correct:** *Running quickly, she felt the finish line seemed far away.* (Clarifies who was running)

Subject-Verb Agreement Errors

The subject and verb in a sentence must agree in number (singular or plural) and person (first, second, or third).

Examples:

- **Singular:** *The dog barks loudly.*
- **Plural:** *The dogs bark loudly.*
- **Person Agreement:** *He runs every morning.* vs. *They run every morning.*

Confusing Words

Some words sound similar but have different meanings and uses. Understanding the difference is key to using them correctly.

Examples:

- *There, Their, They're:*
  - **There:** *Put the book over there.* (refers to a place)
  - **Their:** *Their house is on the corner.* (possessive form)
  - **They're:** *They're going to the park.* (contraction of "they are")
- *Its, It's:*
  - **Its:** *The cat licked its paws.* (possessive form)
  - **It's:** *It's raining outside.* (contraction of "it is")

Double Negatives

Double negatives occur when two negative words are used in the same clause, often creating confusion or an unintended positive meaning.

Examples:

- **Incorrect:** *I don't have no money.* (Means you do have money)
- **Correct:** *I don't have any money.* or *I have no money.*

Punctuation Guidelines:

Punctuation plays a crucial role in clarifying meaning, indicating grammatical structure, and guiding the reader through a text. Understanding punctuation guidelines is essential for effectively communicating ideas in writing. Key punctuation marks and their uses include:

1. Commas

Commas serve multiple purposes, enhancing readability and clarity.

Separating Items in a Series: Use commas to separate items in a list.

- *Example:* I bought apples, oranges, and bananas.

Joining Independent Clauses: Use commas before coordinating conjunctions (and, but, or, nor, for, yet, so) to join independent clauses.

- *Example:* I wanted to go for a walk, but it started to rain.

Setting Off Introductory Elements: Use a comma to set off introductory words, phrases, or clauses at the beginning of a sentence.

- *Example:* After the movie, we went out for dinner.

Separating Nonessential Information: Use commas to set off nonessential information (appositives or nonrestrictive clauses) within a sentence.

- *Example:* My brother, who lives in New York, is visiting us this weekend.

2. Semicolons

Semicolons link closely related ideas and clarify complex lists.

Joining Independent Clauses: Use semicolons to join closely related independent clauses without a coordinating conjunction.

- *Example:* She loves reading; her brother prefers sports.

Separating Items in a Series with Internal Punctuation: Use semicolons to separate items in a series when those items contain internal punctuation.

- *Example:* We visited Paris, France; Rome, Italy; and Berlin, Germany.

3. Colons

Colons introduce additional information and separate explanatory clauses.

Introducing Lists or Explanations: Use colons to introduce lists, explanations, or examples.

- *Example:* Bring the following items: a flashlight, a sleeping bag, and a tent.

Separating Independent Clauses: Separate distinct clauses with a colon when the second clause explains or expands on the first.

- *Example:* She had only one hobby: collecting stamps.

4. Periods

Periods mark the end of sentences and indicate a full stop.

Ending Sentences: Use a period to mark the end of a declarative statement or an imperative sentence.

- *Example:* She finished her homework.

5. Apostrophes

Apostrophes show possession and indicate omitted letters in contractions.

Showing Possession: Use apostrophes to indicate possession or ownership.

- *Example:* This is Sarah's book.

Contracting Words: Use apostrophes in contractions to indicate omitted letters.

- *Example:* Don't forget to call.

6. Quotation Marks

Quotation marks indicate direct speech and enclose titles of short works.

Indicating Direct Speech: Use quotation marks to indicate direct speech or dialogue.

- *Example:* She said, "I'm excited for the trip."

Enclosing Titles or Short Works: Use quotation marks to enclose titles of short works (articles, poems, short stories) or to indicate words used in a special sense.

- *Example:* I just read the article "The Future of Technology."

7. Other Punctuation Marks

These marks add variety and emphasis to writing.

Question Marks: Use question marks to indicate direct questions.

- *Example:* Are you coming to the party?

Exclamation Marks: Use them to express strong emotions or make exclamatory assertions.

- *Example:* Wow, that's amazing!

Parentheses: Include extra information or asides in-between clauses.

- *Example:* She finally answered (after taking five minutes to think) that she would come.

Capitalization Principles:

Correct capitalization is essential for conveying meaning and maintaining clarity in writing. Key principles of capitalization include:

1. Capitalizing Proper Nouns:

Names of People: Capitalize the names of specific individuals, including first names, last names, and titles when used as part of a person's name (e.g., Dr. Smith).

Names of Places: Capitalize the names of specific geographic locations, including countries, cities, states, and landmarks (e.g., New York City, Golden Gate Bridge).

Names of Organizations: Capitalize the names of specific organizations, companies, institutions, and government agencies (e.g., NASA, United Nations).

Titles of Works: Capitalize the titles of books, movies, songs, articles, and other creative works (e.g., *To Kill a Mockingbird*, *Bohemian Rhapsody*).

2. Capitalizing Proper Adjectives:

Derived from Proper Nouns: Capitalize adjectives derived from proper nouns (e.g., American, Shakespearean).

Associated with Geographic Names: Capitalize adjectives associated with geographic names (e.g., African, Parisian).

3. Capitalizing the First Word of a Sentence:

Beginning a Sentence: Capitalize the first word of a complete sentence (e.g., "The sun's bright today.")

4. Capitalizing Major Words in Titles:

Title Case: Capitalize the first and last words of titles and subtitles, as well as all major words in between (e.g., *The Catcher in the Rye*, *An Introduction to Linguistics*).

Strategies for Constructing Clear and Coherent Sentences:

In addition to understanding grammar, punctuation, and capitalization rules, test-takers can employ strategies to construct clear and coherent sentences:

1. Use Parallel Structure

Using parallel structure means ensuring that items in a list or series are grammatically consistent. This enhances readability and provides a rhythm to your writing.

Consistent Form Example:

- **Incorrect:** She likes hiking, to swim, and biking.
- **Correct:** She likes hiking, swimming, and biking.
- **Explanation:** Each item in the list is in the gerund form, making the sentence parallel and easier to read.

2. Maintain Sentence Clarity

Clear and concise language helps convey ideas effectively. Avoiding ambiguity ensures that your sentences are understood as intended.

Clear and Concise Language Example:

- **Incorrect:** Due to the fact that he was late, we missed the bus.
- **Correct:** Because he was late, we missed the bus.
- **Explanation:** The revised sentence is more concise and directly conveys the idea.

Avoid Ambiguity Example:

- **Incorrect:** She saw the man with the telescope.
- **Correct:** She saw the man who had a telescope.
- **Explanation:** The revised sentence clarifies who had the telescope, removing any ambiguity.

3. Check for Subject-Verb Agreement

Ensuring that the subject and verb in a sentence agree in number (singular or plural) is essential for grammatical accuracy.

Agreement in Number Example:

- **Incorrect:** The dogs runs fast.
- **Correct:** The dogs run fast.
- **Explanation:** "Dogs" is plural, so the verb should be "run" to agree in number.

4. Proofread Carefully

Reviewing your writing helps catch and correct errors in grammar, punctuation, capitalization, and sentence structure.

Review Your Writing Example:

- **Original:** The cat were sitting on the mat.
- **Proofread:** The cat was sitting on the mat.
- **Explanation:** Proofreading identified the incorrect verb "were," which was corrected to "was" for subject-verb agreement.

5. Seek Feedback

Getting feedback from peers or instructors can provide valuable insights into areas for improvement in your writing.

Peer Review Example:

- **Original:** I feels tired after running.
- **Feedback:** Correct "feels" to "feel."
- **Explanation:** Peer feedback identified a subject-verb agreement error, improving the sentence.

With dedication, practice, and attention to detail, individuals can improve their language skills and effectively communicate their ideas in writing, ultimately achieving success on the GED exam and beyond.

EFFECTIVE WRITING SKILLS

Effective writing is a critical component of the RLA, as it requires individuals to express their ideas clearly, coherently, and persuasively within the constraints of time and word count. In this extensive guide, we will explore the importance of effective writing skills for the GED exam, strategies for improving writing proficiency, and tips for success in the RLA section.

Understanding the Writing Task

Before delving into strategies for effective writing, it's essential to understand the specific writing tasks you'll encounter on the GED exam. The RLA section typically includes two types of writing tasks:

1. Extended Response (ER) Essay:

Extended Response (ER) essays require test-takers to write an essay responding to a prompt. These prompts may ask individuals to analyze a passage, express their opinions on a given topic, or argue a specific position. In this task, it is essential to develop a clear thesis statement that addresses the prompt and supports it with evidence and examples from the provided text or personal knowledge and experiences.

Crafting an effective ER essay involves careful planning and organization. Begin by analyzing the prompt and identifying key components, such as the main idea, supporting details, and required tasks. Create an outline to structure your response, ensuring that each paragraph focuses on a single main idea and is supported by relevant evidence. Use transitions to guide the reader through your argument and create coherence and cohesion within your essay.

2. Short Answer Response (SAR) Questions:

Short Answer Response (SAR) questions require shorter written responses, typically one or two paragraphs in length. These questions may ask test-takers to summarize a passage, explain a concept, or provide evidence for a particular assertion. While SAR questions are shorter in length, they still require clear and concise writing, supported by evidence from the text or personal knowledge.

When responding to SAR questions, it's essential to read the prompt carefully and identify the specific tasks required. Plan your response by outlining key points and supporting evidence before writing. Aim to provide a focused and coherent answer that directly addresses the prompt while demonstrating your understanding of the text or concept being discussed.

Importance of Effective Writing Skills

Mastering effective writing skills is crucial for success on the GED exam for several reasons:

1. Demonstrating Comprehension:

Effective writing requires a deep understanding of the text or prompt, as well as the ability to analyze and interpret information. By crafting well-written responses, you demonstrate your comprehension of the material and your ability to articulate your thoughts clearly.

When writing essays or responding to questions, take the time to engage with the provided text, identify key themes and ideas, and analyze how they relate to the prompt. Use evidence and examples to support your arguments and demonstrate your understanding of the material.

2. Communicating Ideas Clearly:

Clear and concise writing enables you to communicate your ideas effectively to the reader. Whether you're summarizing a passage, presenting an argument, or explaining a concept, clarity is key to ensuring that your message is understood.

Focus on expressing your ideas in a straightforward and understandable manner. Avoid jargon or overly complex language that may confuse the reader. Use clear and precise language to convey your points, and provide explanations or examples as needed to support your arguments.

3. Supporting Arguments with Evidence:

In both the ER essay and SAR questions, supporting your arguments with evidence is essential. Draw upon the provided text, your own knowledge and experiences, or other relevant sources to bolster your claims.

Be sure to explain how your evidence supports your arguments and why it is significant. Use direct quotations, paraphrases, or summaries from the text to provide specific examples that illustrate your points. Analyze the evidence in relation to your argument, highlighting its relevance and importance to your overall thesis.

4. Organizing Your Thoughts:

Writing coherently requires careful organization of your ideas. Structuring your response with a clear introduction, body paragraphs, and conclusion helps to guide the reader through your argument and ensures that your points are presented logically.

When planning your response, consider the overall structure of your essay or answer. Start with a strong introduction that introduces the topic and provides context for your argument. Develop your main points in the body paragraphs, using evidence to support each claim. Finally, conclude your response by summarizing your key points and restating your thesis in a compelling manner.

5. Demonstrating Writing Proficiency:

The GED exam assesses your ability to write effectively in a variety of contexts, from analyzing texts to presenting arguments. Mastering effective writing skills demonstrates your readiness for further education, employment, and other real-world situations where strong communication skills are essential.

As you prepare for the exam, focus on developing your writing proficiency across different genres and formats. Practice writing essays, short responses, and other written assignments to hone your skills and build confidence in your ability to communicate effectively.

Strategies for Improving Writing Proficiency

Now that we've established the importance of effective writing skills for the GED exam, let's explore some strategies for improving your writing proficiency:

1. Understand the Prompt:

Before you start writing, carefully read and analyze the prompt. Make sure you understand what is being asked of you, whether it's analyzing a passage, expressing your opinion, or providing evidence for a claim. Pay attention to key instructions, such as word count and specific tasks to address.

Take the time to dissect the prompt and identify the main components, including the topic, task, and any specific requirements or guidelines. Consider the purpose of the prompt and what the reader expects from your response. This will help you focus your writing and ensure that you address all aspects of the prompt in your answer.

2. Plan Your Response:

Take a few minutes to plan your response before you begin writing. Consider the critical points you want to make, the evidence to support your arguments, and the overall structure of your response. A clear outline can help you stay focused and organized as you write.

Use brainstorming techniques, such as outlining or clustering, to organize your thoughts and ideas. Identify the key arguments or points you want to address in your response, as well as the evidence or examples you'll use to support them. Create a logical structure for your essay or answer, with clear transitions between ideas and paragraphs.

3. Use Evidence and Examples:

In both the ER essay and SAR questions, supporting your arguments with evidence is essential. Draw upon the provided text, your own knowledge and experiences, or other relevant sources to bolster your claims. Be sure to explain how your evidence supports your arguments and why it is significant.

When incorporating evidence into your writing, be selective and choose the most relevant and compelling examples to support your points. Use a combination of direct quotations, paraphrases, and summaries to provide evidence from the text or other sources. Analyze the evidence in relation to your argument, highlighting its significance and relevance to your thesis.

4. Organize Your Ideas:

Structure your response in a clear and logical manner, with a well-defined introduction, body paragraphs, and conclusion. Segregate your paragraphs by focusing on a singular idea that branches into other discussions in the follow-up passages Use transitions to connect ideas and guide the reader through your response.

Consider the overall flow and coherence of your writing, ensuring that each paragraph builds upon the previous one and leads logically to the next. Use topic sentences to introduce the main idea of each paragraph and provide a clear roadmap for the reader. Use transitions and linking words to create cohesion and ensure that your writing flows smoothly from one point to the next.

5. Be Concise and Clear:

Avoid unnecessary wordiness and ambiguity in your writing. Be concise and get straight to the point, using clear and straightforward language to express your ideas. Aim to convey your message in the most direct and efficient way possible, without sacrificing clarity or depth.

When revising your writing, be ruthless in eliminating unnecessary words or phrases that do not contribute to your argument. Focus on conveying your ideas concisely, using simple and precise terminologies and language that is accessible to your audience. Avoid vague or ambiguous language that may confuse the reader and detract from the clarity of your writing.

6. Revise and Edit:

Take the time to revise carefully and edit your writing. Look out for correct grammar, punctuation, spelling, and syntax. Make sure your writing flows smoothly and that all your ideas are well presented. Consider seeking feedback from a peer or instructor to identify all areas for improvement.

When revising your writing, focus on both macro-level and micro-level aspects of your text. Consider the overall structure and organization of your essay or answer, as well as the clarity and coherence of your arguments. Pay attention to obvious sentence-level issues. They include such issues grammar, punctuation mistakes, and your choice of words. Ensure that your writing is polished and error-free.

CRAFTING YOUR EXTENDED RESPONSE

The Extended Response (ER) section of the GED Reasoning Through Language Arts (RLA) test is designed to assess your ability to construct a well-organized, coherent essay that demonstrates critical thinking and analytical skills. This section requires you to read a prompt, analyze two passages with differing viewpoints, and write an essay that evaluates the arguments and determines which one is better supported by evidence.

Sample Extended Response

Prompt:

You are given two passages that discuss the impact of social media on society. Passage one argues that social media has positively transformed communication and access to information. Passage two contends that social media has led to increased misinformation and negative social consequences.

Passage One:

Social media platforms like Facebook, Twitter, and Instagram have revolutionized how we communicate and access information. These platforms allow for instant communication with friends and family across the globe, fostering stronger relationships. Additionally, social media has democratized information, giving a voice to marginalized groups and allowing for real-time updates on global events. These positive changes have empowered individuals and communities, making the world more connected and informed.

Passage Two:

Despite its benefits, social media has also brought significant negative impacts. The spread of misinformation on platforms like Facebook and Twitter has become a major issue, leading to widespread false beliefs and societal discord. Furthermore, social media can contribute to mental health problems, such as anxiety and depression, due to the pressure to present a perfect life and the comparison with others. These negative consequences often outweigh the benefits, making social media a double-edged sword in modern society.

Sample Extended Response:

Social media's impact on society is a topic of heated debate. While both passages present compelling arguments, the argument in Passage One is better supported by evidence and offers a more comprehensive view of social media's transformative effects.

Passage One effectively highlights the positive changes brought about by social media. It emphasizes the ability of platforms like Facebook, Twitter, and Instagram to facilitate instant communication, which has helped strengthen relationships across distances. For instance, people can now stay connected with family and friends around the world, sharing updates and experiences in real-time. This global connectivity fosters a sense of community and belonging, which is a significant positive outcome.

Moreover, Passage One discusses how social media has democratized information, providing a platform for marginalized voices. This is evident in movements like #MeToo and Black Lives Matter, where social media played a crucial role in raising awareness and mobilizing support. These platforms have allowed individuals to share their stories and experiences, creating a more informed and engaged public. The real-time updates on global events, such as natural disasters or political movements, also underscore the importance of social media in disseminating crucial information quickly and efficiently.

On the other hand, Passage Two raises valid concerns about the negative impacts of social media, particularly the spread of misinformation and its effect on mental health. It is true that misinformation can spread rapidly on social media, leading to confusion and mistrust. However, this issue can be mitigated through better regulation and the implementation of fact-checking mechanisms by social media companies. The argument in Passage Two, while important, does not outweigh the significant benefits outlined in Passage One.

Furthermore, the mental health issues associated with social media, such as anxiety and depression, are real concerns. Nevertheless, these issues are not solely caused by social media but are part of a broader societal problem that includes other factors like economic stress and personal relationships. Social media can also be used to provide support and resources for those struggling with mental health issues, offering communities and networks for individuals to seek help.

In conclusion, while social media does have its drawbacks, the argument presented in Passage One is more compelling and well-supported. The transformative power of social media in enhancing communication, democratizing information, and fostering global connectivity far outweighs the negative aspects highlighted in Passage Two. Social media, when used responsibly, has the potential to continue making significant positive contributions to society.

Step-by-Step Breakdown of the Sample Extended Response

Step 1: Understand the Prompt

The first step is to carefully read and understand the prompt. For this example, the prompt asks you to analyze two passages discussing the impact of social media on society and determine which argument is better supported by evidence.

Prompt Summary:

- Passage One: Argues that social media has positively transformed communication and access to information.
- Passage Two: Argues that social media has led to increased misinformation and negative social consequences.

Step 2: Plan Your Response

Before writing, plan your essay. Identify the main points of each passage, decide which argument is stronger, and outline your response structure.

Outline:

1. Introduction: State your position and briefly mention the key points.
2. Body Paragraph 1: Summarize and analyze the argument in Passage One.
3. Body Paragraph 2: Summarize and analyze the argument in Passage Two.
4. Body Paragraph 3: Compare the arguments and explain why Passage One is stronger.
5. Conclusion: Restate your position and summarize your analysis.

Step 3: Write the Introduction

The introduction should clearly state your thesis and provide a brief overview of the arguments.

Introduction Example: "Social media's impact on society is a topic of heated debate. While both passages present compelling arguments, the argument in Passage One is better supported by evidence and offers a more comprehensive view of social media's transformative effects."

Explanation: The introduction sets the stage by acknowledging the debate and clearly stating that Passage One has a stronger argument.

Step 4: Write the Body Paragraphs

Each body paragraph should focus on summarizing and analyzing one passage, followed by a comparison.

Body Paragraph 1: Passage One Analysis "Passage One effectively highlights the positive changes brought about by social media. It emphasizes the ability of platforms like Facebook, Twitter, and Instagram to facilitate instant communication, which has helped strengthen relationships across distances. For instance, people can now stay connected with family and friends around the world, sharing updates and experiences in real-time. This global connectivity fosters a sense of community and belonging, which is a significant positive outcome."

Explanation: This paragraph summarizes Passage One's main points and provides examples of how social media positively impacts communication and relationships.

Body Paragraph 2: Passage Two Analysis "Passage Two raises valid concerns about the negative impacts of social media, particularly the spread of misinformation and its effect on mental health. It is true that misinformation can spread rapidly on social media, leading to confusion and mistrust. However, this issue can be mitigated through better regulation and the implementation of fact-checking mechanisms by social media companies. The argument in Passage Two, while important, does not outweigh the significant benefits outlined in Passage One."

Explanation: This paragraph summarizes Passage Two's main points, acknowledges its concerns, and begins to compare the arguments by suggesting solutions to the issues raised.

Body Paragraph 3: Comparison and Analysis "Furthermore, the mental health issues associated with social media, such as anxiety and depression, are real concerns. Nevertheless, these issues are not solely caused by social media but are part of a broader societal problem that includes other factors like economic stress and personal relationships. Social media can also be used to provide support and resources for those struggling with mental health issues, offering communities and networks for individuals to seek help."

Explanation: This paragraph continues the comparison, highlighting the broader context of the issues raised in Passage Two and emphasizing the supportive role social media can play.

Step 5: Write the Conclusion

The conclusion should restate your thesis and summarize your main points.

Conclusion Example: "In conclusion, while social media does have its drawbacks, the argument presented in Passage One is more compelling and well-supported. The transformative power of social media in enhancing communication, democratizing information, and fostering global connectivity far outweighs the negative aspects highlighted in Passage Two. Social media, when used responsibly, has the potential to continue making significant positive contributions to society."

Explanation: The conclusion restates the thesis that Passage One is stronger and summarizes the key reasons why, reinforcing the overall argument.

PART IV
MATHEMATICAL REASONING

Mathematical reasoning is a fundamental component of the GED test, designed to evaluate your ability to apply mathematical concepts and solve problems in various contexts. Whether you're doing further studies, advancing your career, or personal development, a strong foundation in mathematical reasoning is essential. This section will explore the key aspects of mathematical reasoning tested in the GED exam, providing insights and strategies to help you effectively prepare.

BASIC MATH SKILLS FOR THE GED TEST

Arithmetic Skills

Arithmetic lays the groundwork for mathematical reasoning and problem-solving. It encompasses fundamental operations, including addition of numbers, subtraction, simple multiplication, and division. Mastery of arithmetic skills is crucial for performing calculations efficiently and accurately on the GED test. Here's an overview of key arithmetic skills:

Addition and Subtraction

Addition involves combining two or more numbers to find their sum, while subtraction entails finding the difference between two numbers. Practice adding and subtracting whole numbers, decimals, and fractions to build fluency in these operations.

Addition of Whole Numbers:

- Example: $25 + 37 = 62$

Subtraction of Whole Numbers:

- Example: $82 - 19 = 63$

Addition of Decimals:

- Example: $4.75 + 3.60 = 8.35$

Subtraction of Decimals:

- Example: $9.50 - 2.25 = 7.25$

Addition of Fractions:

- Example: $2/3 + 1/4 = 8/12 + 3/12 = 11/12$

Subtraction of Fractions:

- Example: $5/6 - 1/3 = 5/6 - 2/6 = 3/6 = 1/2$

Multiplication and Division

Multiplication involves repeated addition, while division involves sharing or partitioning a quantity into equal parts. Practice multiplying and dividing whole numbers, decimals, and fractions, and understand the relationship between these operations.

Multiplication of Whole Numbers:

- Example: 12 x 7 = 84

Division of Whole Numbers:

- Example: 56 ÷ 8 = 7

Multiplication of Decimals:

- Example: 3.4 x 2.5 = 8.5

Division of Decimals:

- Example: 9.6 ÷ 1.2 = 8

Multiplication of Fractions:

- Example: 3/4 x 2/5 = 6/20 = 3/10

Division of Fractions:

- Example: 3/4 ÷ 2/5 = 3/4 x 5/2 = 15/8

Fractions, Decimals, and Percentages

Understanding fractions, decimals, and percentages is essential for solving a wide range of math problems. Learn how to convert between fractions, decimals, and percentages, and perform operations involving these forms.

Converting Fractions to Decimals:

- Example: 3/4 = 0.75

Converting Decimals to Percentages:

- Example: 0.75 x 100 = 75%

Converting Percentages to Fractions:

- Example: 75% = 75/100 = 3/4

Order of Operations

Familiarize yourself with the order of operations (PEMDAS: Parentheses, Exponents, Multiplication and Division, Addition and Subtraction) to correctly evaluate mathematical expressions and equations.

Example:

- Solve $7 + 3 \times (10 - 4)^2 \div 2$
- Step-by-Step:
  - Parentheses: $10 - 4 = 6$
  - Exponents: $6^2 = 36$
  - Multiplication/Division (left to right): $3 \times 36 = 108$
  - Division: $108 \div 2 = 54$
  - Addition: $7 + 54 = 61$

Estimation

Develop the ability to estimate quantities and approximate solutions to mathematical problems. Estimation skills are valuable for quickly checking the reasonableness of answers on the GED test.

Example:

- Estimate 47×6
- Rounded Numbers: $50 \times 6 = 300$
- Approximate Answer: 300

Algebra Skills

Algebraic skills involve the manipulation of symbols and expressions to solve equations and inequalities. Understanding algebraic concepts is essential for solving more complex problems on the GED test. Here are some key algebraic skills to focus on, along with examples and common equations to remember:

Solving Equations

Learn techniques for solving linear equations and inequalities such as one-step, two-step, and even complex multi-step equations. Understand the properties of equality and apply them to isolate variables.

One-Step Equations:

- Example: $x + 5 = 12$
- Solution: Subtract 5 from both sides: $x = 12 - 5$, so $x = 7$

Two-Step Equations:

- Example: $3x - 4 = 11$
- Solution: Add 4 to both sides: $3x = 15$. Then divide by 3: $x = 5$

Multi-Step Equations:

- Example: $2(x - 3) + 4 = 10$
- Solution: Distribute the 2: $2x - 6 + 4 = 10$. Combine like terms: $2x - 2 = 10$. Add 2 to both sides: $2x = 12$. Divide by 2: $x = 6$

Common Equations to Remember:

- Linear equation: $ax + b = c$
- Inequality: $ax + b < c$ or $ax + b > c$

Graphing Linear Equations

Graph linear equations on the coordinate plane and interpret the slope and intercepts of a line. Understand how to determine the slope between points and use it to graph linear equations.

Slope-Intercept Form:

- Equation: $y = mx + b$
- Example: $y = 2x + 3$
- Graphing: Plot the y-intercept $(0, 3)$, and use the slope $m = 2$ (rise over run) to plot another point. Draw the line through these points.

Finding Slope Between Points:

- Formula: $m = (y_2 - y_1) / (x_2 - x_1)$
- Example: Points $(1, 2)$ and $(3, 6)$
- Calculation: $m = (6 - 2) / (3 - 1) = 4 / 2 = 2$

Systems of Equations

Know how to solve linear equation systems using substitution, elimination, or graphing methods. Understand the concept of a solution to a system of equations and how it relates to the intersection of lines on the coordinate plane.

Substitution Method:

- Example: $y = 2x + 3$ and $x + y = 5$
- Solution: Substitute $y = 2x + 3$ into the second equation: $x + 2x + 3 = 5$, which simplifies to $3x + 3 = 5$. Solving for x gives $x = 2/3$. Then substitute back to find y.

Elimination Method:

- Example: $2x + 3y = 6$ and $4x - 3y = 12$
- Solution: Add the two equations to eliminate y: $6x = 18$, thus $x = 3$. Substitute x back to find y.

Common Equations to Remember:

- System of equations:
  - $ax + by = c$
  - $dx + ey = f$

Quadratic Equations

Familiarize yourself with quadratic equations and their properties, including vertex form, standard form, and factored form. Learn how to solve quadratic equations by factoring, completing the square, and using the quadratic formula.

Standard Form:

- Equation: $ax^2 + bx + c = 0$
- Example: $x^2 - 5x + 6 = 0$
- Factoring: $(x - 2)(x - 3) = 0$, so $x = 2$ or $x = 3$

Quadratic Formula:

- Formula: $x = (-b \pm \sqrt{(b^2 - 4ac)}) / 2a$
- Example: For $x^2 - 4x - 5 = 0$, $a = 1$, $b = -4$, $c = -5$
- Solution: $x = (4 \pm \sqrt{(16 + 20)}) / 2 = (4 \pm \sqrt{36}) / 2 = (4 \pm 6) / 2$, so $x = 5$ or $x = -1$

Polynomials

Understand the structure of polynomials and learn the addition, subtraction, multiplication, and division of polynomials. Practice simplifying polynomial expressions and identifying their degree and leading coefficient.

Addition/Subtraction:

- Example: $(3x^2 + 2x + 1) + (2x^2 - x + 4) = 5x^2 + x + 5$

Multiplication:

- Example: $(x + 2)(x - 3) = x^2 - 3x + 2x - 6 = x^2 - x - 6$

Identifying Degree and Leading Coefficient:

- Example: For the polynomial $4x^3 + 3x^2 - 2x + 7$, the degree is 3 and the leading coefficient is 4

Geometry Skills

Geometry involves the study of shapes, sizes, and spatial relationships. Geometry skills are essential for solving problems involving angles, lines, triangles, polygons, circles, and three-dimensional figures. Here's an overview of key geometry skills for the GED test, with better explanations and examples:

Basic Geometric Shapes

Identify and classify geometric shapes, including points, circles, lines, angles, and polygons. Understand the properties of these shapes and their relationships.

- **Points:** A location in space without size or dimension.
- **Lines:** Straight one-dimensional figures extending infinitely in both directions.
- **Circles:** All points equidistant from a center point.
- **Angles:** Formed by two rays with a common endpoint (vertex).
- **Polygons:** Closed figures with three or more straight sides.

Example: A triangle (polygon) has three sides and three angles.

Properties of Angles and Lines

Learn about different types of angles and lines. Understand angle relationships, such as complementary, supplementary, and vertical angles.

Types of Angles:

- **Acute Angle:** Less than 90 degrees.
- **Right Angle:** Exactly 90 degrees.
- **Obtuse Angle:** Greater than 90 degrees but less than 180 degrees.

Types of Lines:

- **Parallel Lines:** Lines that never intersect.
- **Perpendicular Lines:** Lines that intersect at a right angle.

Example: Two angles that add up to 90 degrees are complementary, such as 30 degrees and 60 degrees.

Triangle Properties

Understand the properties of triangles, including angles, side lengths, and types of triangles. Learn about the Pythagorean theorem and how to apply it in finding missing side lengths in right triangles.

Types of Triangles:

- **Equilateral:** All sides and angles are equal.
- **Isosceles:** Two sides and two angles are equal.
- **Scalene:** All sides and angles are different.
- **Right Triangle:** One angle is 90 degrees.

Pythagorean Theorem: $a^2 + b^2 = c^2$ (where c is the hypotenuse).

Example: For a right triangle with sides 3 and 4, the hypotenuse is $sqrt(3^2 + 4^2) = sqrt(9 + 16) = 5$.

Quadrilaterals and Polygons

Identify and classify quadrilaterals and polygons based on their properties. Learn about the sum of interior angles in polygons and apply it to solve problems involving regular polygons.

Types of Quadrilaterals:

- **Square:** All sides equal, all angles 90 degrees.
- **Rectangle:** Opposite sides equal, all angles 90 degrees.
- **Parallelogram:** Opposite sides and angles equal.
- **Rhombus:** All sides equal, opposite angles equal.
- **Trapezoid:** At least one pair of parallel sides.

Sum of Interior Angles Formula: (n-2) * 180 degrees, where n is the number of sides.

Example: For a hexagon (6 sides), the sum of interior angles is (6-2) * 180 = 720 degrees.

Circles

Understand the properties of circles, including radius, diameter, circumference, and area. Learn how to calculate the circumference and area of a circle using appropriate formulas.

- **Radius (r):** Distance from the center to any point on the circle.
- **Diameter (d):** Twice the radius (d = 2r).
- **Circumference (C):** $C = 2\pi r$ or $C = \pi d$.
- **Area (A):** $A = \pi r^2$.

Example: For a circle with a radius of 4, the circumference is $2\pi * 4 = 8\pi$ and the area is $\pi * 4^2 = 16\pi$.

Three-Dimensional Figures

Identify and classify figures such as prisms, pyramids, cylinders, cones, and spheres. Understand how to calculate the volume and surface area of these figures using appropriate formulas.

Prism:

- Volume (V) = Base Area * Height

Pyramid:

- Volume (V) = (1/3) * Base Area * Height

Cylinder:

- Volume (V) = πr^2h
- Surface Area (SA) = 2πrh + 2πr^2

Cone:

- Volume (V) = (1/3)πr^2h
- Surface Area (SA) = πr(r + sqrt(h^2 + r^2))

Sphere:

- Volume (V) = (4/3)πr^3
- Surface Area (SA) = 4πr^2

Example: For a cylinder with a radius of 3 and height of 5, the volume is π * 3^2 * 5 = 45π and the surface area is 2π * 3 * 5 + 2π * 3^2 = 30π + 18π = 48π.

Data Analysis Skills

Data analysis involves interpreting and analyzing information presented in various formats, such as tables, charts, graphs, and statistics. Data analysis skills are essential for solving problems involving numerical and graphical data. Explored further in detail later, here's a brief overview of what you need to know about data analysis for the GED test:

Interpreting Graphical Data: Learn how to read and interpret different types of graphs, including bar graphs, line graphs, pie charts, and scatterplots. Understand how to extract information from graphs and draw conclusions based on the data presented.

Analyzing Statistics: Understand basic statistical concepts such as mean, median, mode, range, and standard deviation. Learn how to calculate these measures and interpret their significance in different contexts.

Probability: Understand the concept of probability and its applications in predicting outcomes of events. Learn how to calculate probabilities of simple and compound events and understand the relationship between probability and odds.

Descriptive and Inferential Statistics: Differentiate between descriptive statistics (summarizing and describing data) and inferential statistics (making predictions or inferences based on data). Understand the purpose and use of each type of statistic in data analysis.

Problem-Solving Techniques

Problem-solving skills are essential for tackling complex math problems effectively. Developing problem-solving techniques can help you approach unfamiliar problems with confidence and find solutions efficiently. Here are some strategies for honing your problem-solving skills:

Understand the Problem: Read the problem carefully and make sure you understand what is being asked. Identify the given information as well as the unstated assumptions in the problem.

Plan a Solution: Develop a plan or strategy for solving the problem based on the information given. Decide on the appropriate mathematical operations or methods to use and outline the steps you will take to reach the solution.

Execute the Plan: Implement your chosen strategy to solve the problem, performing calculations accurately and systematically. Keep things neat; label each step and explain necessary choices.

Check Your Solution: After finding a solution, review your work carefully to ensure its accuracy and completeness. Check your answer against the given information and verify that it makes sense in the context of the problem.

Practice Regularly: Practice solving a variety of math problems regularly to build confidence and proficiency. Work on problems from different topics and difficulty levels to strengthen your skills and expand your problem-solving abilities.

You can build the confidence and competence needed to succeed on the math section of the GED test by focusing on these fundamental math skills and practicing regularly. Whether you're aiming to obtain your high school equivalency diploma or pursue further education and career opportunities, mastering these basic math skills will serve you well in achieving your goals

ALGEBRAIC THINKING

Algebraic thinking is a crucial component of the GED test, encompassing a range of skills and concepts that are essential for solving mathematical problems and reasoning quantitatively. This guide will provide an in-depth exploration of algebraic thinking in the context of the GED test, covering key topics such as solving equations, understanding functions, interpreting graphs, and applying algebraic concepts to real-world scenarios.

Understanding Algebraic Expressions

Algebraic expressions are mathematical expressions that contain variables, constants, and mathematical operations. They represent relationships between quantities and can be manipulated and evaluated to solve problems. Understanding algebraic expressions is essential for interpreting and solving algebraic equations and inequalities on the GED test.

Algebraic expressions can take various forms, including linear, quadratic, polynomial, and exponential expressions. Each type of expression has its own properties and characteristics, which determine how it behaves when manipulated. By familiarizing yourself with the different types of algebraic expressions and their properties, you can develop the skills needed to solve a wide range of algebraic problems on the GED test.

Examples of Algebraic Expressions

1. Linear Expression:

- $3x + 5$
- This expression is linear because it represents a straight line when graphed. It consists of a variable term ($3x$) and a constant (5).

2. Quadratic Expression:

- $2x^2 - 4x + 1$
- This expression is quadratic because it includes a squared term (x^2). Quadratic expressions form parabolas when graphed.

3. Polynomial Expression:

- $4x^3 - 3x^2 + 2x - 7$
- This expression is a polynomial of degree 3 (cubic) because it has a term with x^3. Polynomial expressions can have multiple terms with varying degrees.

Solving Equations and Inequalities

Solving equations and inequalities is a central aspect of algebraic thinking, requiring the application of algebraic techniques to find the values of unknown variables. Equations and inequalities represent relationships between quantities and can be solved using various methods, including substitution, elimination, graphing, and algebraic manipulation.

When solving equations and inequalities on the GED test, it's essential to follow a systematic approach and carefully track each step of the solution process. Start by identifying the given information and the unknowns, then choose an appropriate method for solving the equation or inequality based on its structure and complexity. Work through the problem methodically, performing the necessary algebraic operations to isolate the variable and find its value.

Examples of Solving Equations and Inequalities

1. Solving Linear Equations:

- Example: $2x + 3 = 11$
- Solution: Subtract 3 from both sides: $2x = 8$, then divide by 2: $x = 4$

2. Solving Quadratic Equations:

- Example: $x^2 - 5x + 6 = 0$
- Solution: Factor the equation: $(x - 2)(x - 3) = 0$, then set each factor to zero: $x = 2$ or $x = 3$

3. Solving Inequalities:

- Example: $3x - 4 < 5$
- Solution: Add 4 to both sides: $3x < 9$, then divide by 3: $x < 3$

Understanding Functions and Relations

Functions are mathematical relationships that assign each input value to exactly one output value. They can be represented algebraically, graphically, or verbally and are used to model a wide range of real-world phenomena. Understanding functions and relations is essential for analyzing mathematical patterns, making predictions, and solving problems on the GED test.

Functions can take various forms, including linear, quadratic, exponential, and trigonometric functions. Each type of function has its own characteristics, such as slope, intercepts, domain, and range, which determine its behavior and properties. By studying the properties of different types of functions and their graphical representations, you can develop the skills needed to analyze functions and solve problems involving them on the GED test.

Examples of Functions and Relations

1. Linear Functions:

- Example: $f(x) = 2x + 3$
- Characteristics: The graph is a straight line with a slope of 2 and a y-intercept of 3. The domain and range are both all real numbers.

2. Quadratic Functions:

- Example: $f(x) = x^2 - 4x + 4$
- Characteristics: The graph is a parabola that opens upwards. The vertex is at (2, 0), and the domain is all real numbers, while the range is $y \geq 0$.

3. Exponential Functions:

- Example: $f(x) = 2^x$
- Characteristics: The graph shows exponential growth, with a horizontal asymptote at $y = 0$. The domain is all real numbers, and the range is $y > 0$.

Interpreting Graphs and Tables

Graphs and tables are powerful tools for representing mathematical relationships and visualizing data. They provide valuable insights into patterns, trends, and relationships between variables, making them essential for interpreting and analyzing information on the GED test.

When interpreting graphs and tables on the GED test, it's important to pay attention to key features such as the shape of the graph, the direction of the trend, and the relationship between variables. Identify any patterns or trends in the data and consider how they relate to the problem at hand. Use the information provided in the graph or table to make predictions, draw conclusions, or solve problems based on the given data.

Applying Algebraic Concepts to Real-World Scenarios

Algebraic concepts are not only used to solve abstract mathematical problems but also to model and solve real-world scenarios. By applying algebraic thinking to real-world situations, you can analyze problems, make predictions, and formulate solutions to practical problems encountered in everyday life.

Real-world scenarios involving algebraic thinking may include problems related to finance, economics, science, engineering, or social sciences. These problems often require you to translate verbal descriptions into algebraic expressions or equations, apply mathematical models to analyze data, and interpret the results in the context of the problem. By developing the ability to apply algebraic concepts to real-world scenarios, you can demonstrate your proficiency in algebraic thinking on the GED test and beyond.

Forming Algebraic Equations from Real-World Scenarios

Here are examples showing how to form algebraic equations from the given word problems:

1. Finance:

- **Problem:** Sarah wants to save for a new laptop that costs $800. She already has $200 saved and plans to save an additional $50 each week. How many weeks will it take Sarah to save enough money to buy the laptop?
- **Equation:** Let ww represent the number of weeks. The equation is $200 + 50w = 800$.

2. Economics:

- **Problem:** A company produces widgets and sells them for $15 each. The fixed costs for production are $2000, and the variable cost per widget is $5. How many widgets must the company sell to break even?
- **Equation:** Let xx represent the number of widgets. The equation is $15x = 2000 + 5x$.

3. Science:

- **Problem:** The speed of sound in air is approximately 343 meters per second. If a thunderclap is heard 5 seconds after a lightning flash is seen, how far away is the storm?
- **Equation:** Let dd represent the distance. The equation is $d = 343 * 5$.

4. Engineering:

- **Problem:** A rectangular garden has a length that is 3 meters more than twice its width. If the perimeter of the garden is 54 meters, what are the dimensions of the garden?
- **Equation:** Let ww represent the width. Then the length ll is $2w + 3$. The perimeter equation is $2w + 2(2w + 3) = 54$.

5. Social Sciences:

- **Problem:** The population of a small town is currently 15,000 and is growing at a rate of 2% per year. What will the population be in 5 years?
- **Equation:** Let PP represent the population. The equation is $P = 15000 * (1 + 0.02)^5$.

6. Personal Finance:

- **Problem:** John takes out a loan of $10,000 with an annual interest rate of 5%, compounded annually. How much will he owe after 3 years?
- **Equation:** Let A represent the amount owed. The equation is $A = 10000 * (1 + 0.05)^3$.

7. Logistics:

- **Problem:** A delivery truck travels at an average speed of 60 miles per hour. If the truck has already traveled 120 miles and needs to cover a total distance of 300 miles, how much longer will the journey take?
- **Equation:** Let t represent the time in hours. The remaining distance is 300 - 120, so the equation is $60t = 180$.

Strategies for Success in Algebraic Thinking

To excel in algebraic thinking on the GED test, it's important to develop strong problem-solving skills, mathematical reasoning abilities, and a deep understanding of algebraic concepts. Try out the following strategies:

1. **Practice Regularly:** Consistent practice is the cornerstone of success in algebraic thinking. Allocate dedicated time to tackle algebraic problems regularly, focusing on diverse topics and difficulty levels. Utilize resources such as practice tests, worksheets, and online platforms to access a wide range of problems. Regular practice not only reinforces your understanding of algebraic concepts but also enhances your problem-solving skills and builds confidence in approaching different types of questions on the GED test.

2. **Understand Concepts:** Instead of memorizing formulas and procedures, strive to grasp the underlying concepts behind algebraic expressions, equations, functions, and graphs. Take the time to explore the principles governing each concept and understand how they relate to real-world scenarios. Utilize visual aids, examples, and explanations to deepen your understanding and develop a solid foundation in algebraic thinking. By understanding the why behind each concept, you can better apply them to solve problems creatively and adapt to unfamiliar situations on the GED test.

3. **Review Basic Skills:** Mastery of basic algebraic skills is essential for tackling more complex problems on the GED test. Ensure proficiency in fundamental skills such as solving equations, graphing functions, interpreting graphs and tables, and manipulating algebraic expressions. Review key concepts and techniques regularly, focusing on areas where you may need additional practice or reinforcement. Strengthening your basic skills provides a solid framework upon which you can build more advanced algebraic thinking abilities, ultimately enhancing your performance on the GED test.

4. **Use Resources Wisely:** Take advantage of a variety of resources to support your preparation for the algebraic thinking section of the GED test. Explore study guides, textbooks, online tutorials, and instructional videos to gain insights into algebraic concepts and problem-solving strategies. Additionally, make use of practice tests and sample questions to understand the format and types of questions you may encounter on the GED test. Utilize resources that cater to your learning style and preferences, whether it's visual, auditory, or hands-on, to maximize your understanding and retention of algebraic concepts.

5. **Seek Assistance Where Necessary:** Don't hesitate to seek advice from teachers, tutors, peers, or online communities when you have questions about specific algebraic concepts or problems. Reach out for clarification, guidance, or additional resources to address areas of difficulty and deepen your understanding. Collaborate with peers to discuss strategies, share insights, and work through problems together. By seeking help when needed and engaging in collaborative learning, you can overcome obstacles more effectively and accelerate your progress in mastering algebraic thinking for the GED test.

Incorporating these strategies into your preparation regimen can significantly enhance your readiness and performance in the algebraic thinking section of the GED test. By practicing regularly, understanding underlying concepts, reviewing basic skills, utilizing resources wisely, and seeking help when needed, you can build confidence, strengthen your problem-solving abilities, and achieve success on the GED test and beyond.

DATA ANALYSIS, STATISTICS, AND PROBABILITY

Interpreting Graphs and Charts

Data is often represented visually using graphs and charts. On the GED test, you may encounter bar graphs, line graphs, pie charts, and scatter plots. Each type presents data uniquely, and understanding how to interpret these visuals is crucial.

- **Bar Graphs:** Compare quantities across different categories.
- **Line Graphs:** Show changes over time.
- **Pie Charts:** Display proportions of a whole.
- **Scatter Plots:** Illustrate relationships between two variables.

Example: You might be given a bar graph showing sales figures for different products and asked to identify which product had the highest sales.

Analyzing Data Sets

Data sets can range from simple lists of numbers to complex tables. Analyzing these sets involves identifying measures of central tendency like mean, median, and mode, which are measures of average. It also includes understanding the spread of data, such as range and standard deviation, which indicate variability within the data set.

- **Mean:** The average of the data set.
- **Median:** The middle value when the data set is ordered.
- **Mode:** The most frequently occurring value.
- **Range:** The difference between the highest and lowest values.

Example: Given a list of test scores, you might be asked to calculate the mean score.

The Role of Statistics

Statistics is the science of gathering, evaluating, presenting, and organizing data. In the context of the GED test, statistics helps in understanding how data can be used to support arguments or hypotheses.

- **Descriptive Statistics:** Summarize data from a sample using measures of central tendency and variability.
- **Inferential Statistics:** Make predictions or inferences about a population based on a sample of data, involving hypothesis testing, confidence intervals, and significance levels.

Example: You might analyze survey data to infer the preferences of a larger population.

Probability Fundamentals

Probability measures the likelihood that an event will occur, quantified as a number between 0 (impossibility) and 1 (certainty). The GED test includes questions on basic probability concepts and calculations.

- **Calculating Simple Probability:** Divide the number of favorable outcomes by the total number of possible outcomes.

Example: The probability of rolling a 3 on a six-sided die is 1/6.

- **Compound Events and the Addition Rule:** Involves the combination of two or more simple events. The addition rule helps calculate the chance of either of two mutually exclusive events occurring.

Example: The probability of drawing a heart or a diamond from a deck of cards is 13/52 + 13/52 = 1/2.

Statistical Reasoning

Statistical reasoning involves interpreting data and making decisions based on statistical methods, including evaluating the strength of evidence and making predictions.

- **Correlation vs. Causation:** A correlation between two variables does not imply that one causes the other. The GED test may present scenarios where you must discern whether a relationship between variables suggests causation or merely correlation.

Example: A graph showing a correlation between ice cream sales and crime rates does not imply that ice cream sales cause crime.

- **Evaluating Statistical Claims:** Consider the source of the data, the sample size, and the methods used to collect and analyze the data to determine the validity and reliability of statistical findings.

Example: Critically evaluate a study claiming a new drug is effective, considering the sample size and study design.

Grasping Probability Concepts

Probability is a fundamental aspect of the GED Mathematical Reasoning test. It involves understanding and calculating the likelihood of various outcomes.

- **Basic Probability:** Measures how likely it is for an event to occur. Stated as a number between 0 and 1.

Example: There is a 1/2 chance that a coin will land on heads when flipped.

- **Probability of Multiple Events:** When dealing with multiple events, understand how to calculate the combined probability. If two events are independent, the likelihood of both happening equals the product of their individual probabilities.

Example: The probability of flipping two coins and both landing on heads is 1/2 * 1/2 = 1/4.

GEOMETRY AND MEASUREMENT

Introduction to Geometry and Measurement

Geometry deals with the properties of shapes and sizes, their relationships, and measurements. It encompasses concepts such as points, circles, lines, polygons, angles, and three-dimensional figures, among others. Measurement, on the other hand, involves quantifying dimensions, lengths, areas, volumes, and angles of geometric objects. Together, geometry and measurement provide a framework for understanding the physical world and solving problems involving spatial relationships and quantities.

Key Concepts in Geometry

Geometry on the GED test covers a wide range of topics, including basic shapes, angles, lines, triangles, quadrilaterals, circles, and three-dimensional figures. Understanding these basic concepts is a requirement for solving geometry problems and reasoning geometrically. Below are detailed explanations of some fundamental concepts in geometry:

Points, Lines, and Angles: A point is a location in space without dimension or size. A line is a straight path extending infinitely in both directions. An angle is forms when two rays share an endpoint, commonly known as the vertex. The measurement of angles is done in degrees. E.g., a full circle containing 360 degrees.

Polygons: A closed plane figure formed by three or more segments of line known as sides. Common polygons you should know include triangles (those with 3 sides), quadrilaterals (having 4 sides), pentagons (5 sides), hexagons (6 sided), and so on. Note also that polygons are classified depending on the number of sides and angles they possess.

Triangles: Triangles are polygons with three angles and sides. They can be categorized according to angles (acute, obtuse, right) or side lengths (equilateral, isosceles, scalene). A triangle's internal angles always add up to 180 degrees.

Quadrilaterals: Polygons having four sides and four angles are called quadrilaterals. Quadrilaterals can be squares, rectangles, parallelograms, rhombuses, or trapezoids. Each type of quadrilateral has unique properties and characteristics.

Circles: A circle is made up of all the points in a plane that are equally spaced out from the center, which is a fixed point. The diameter is the length of the circle that passes through the center, while the radius is the distance from the center to any point on the circle. A circle's area is the measurement of the space it encloses, while its circumference is the distance around its perimeter.

Three-Dimensional Figures: Solids, or three-dimensional figures, are defined by their length, breadth, and height. Examples include prisms, pyramids, cylinders, cones, and spheres. Each type of solid has unique properties, such as the number of faces, edges, and vertices, as well as formulas for calculating volume and surface area.

Key Concepts in Measurement

Measurement involves quantifying the dimensions, lengths, areas, volumes, and angles of geometric objects. Understanding measurement concepts and techniques is essential for solving problems involving quantities and spatial relationships. Below are detailed explanations of some fundamental concepts in measurement:

Length and Distance: Length is the measurement of an object's length, which is often stated in measures like inches, feet, meters, or miles. The separation between two points is expressed as their distance from one another. Techniques for measuring length and distance include rulers, tape measures, and formulas for calculating distances between points in coordinate geometry.

Area: Area is the amount of space enclosed by a two-dimensional shape. Square inches, feet, or meters are some examples of the units used to measure it. Based on its dimensions, the area of a shape can be computed using the relevant formulas. Common shapes for which area is calculated include rectangles, triangles, circles, and irregular polygons. Based on its dimensions, the area of a shape can be computed using the relevant formulas.

Rectangle:

- Area = length × width

Triangle:

- Area = 1/2 × base × height

Circle:

- Area = π × radius^2

Trapezoid:

- Area = 1/2 × (base1 + base2) × height

Parallelogram:

- Area = base × height

Volume: Volume is the amount of space enclosed by a three-dimensional object. It is measured in cubic units, such as cubic inches, cubic feet, or cubic meters. A solid's volume can be determined using proper formulas based on its dimensions. Common solids for which volume is calculated include prisms, pyramids, cylinders, cones, and spheres. A solid's volume can be determined using proper formulas based on its dimensions.

Rectangular Prism:

- Volume = length × width × height

Cylinder:

- Volume = π × radius^2 × height

Cone:

- Volume = 1/3 × π × radius^2 × height

Sphere:

- Volume = 4/3 × π × radius^3

Pyramid:

- Volume = 1/3 × base area × height

Angle Measurement: A complete circle has 360 degrees, and angles are expressed in degrees. Techniques for measuring angles include protractors, angle rulers, and geometric principles such as the properties of complementary, supplementary, and vertical angles. Angles can also be classified based on their measures, such as acute (less than 90 degrees), obtuse (greater than 90 degrees), or right (exactly 90 degrees).

1. Sum of Interior Angles of a Polygon:

- Sum of interior angles = (n - 2) × 180 degrees, where n is the number of sides

2. Complementary Angles:

- Two angles whose measures add up to 90 degrees

3. Supplementary Angles:

- Two angles whose measures add up to 180 degrees

Perimeter: Perimeter is the distance around the boundary of a two-dimensional shape. To calculate it, add the lengths of the shape's sides. Perimeter is often measured in the same units as length, such as inches, feet, or meters. Techniques for measuring perimeter include rulers, tape measures, and formulas for calculating the sum of side lengths. To calculate it, add the lengths of the shape's sides.

Rectangle:

- Perimeter = 2 × (length + width)

Square:

- Perimeter = 4 × side

Triangle:

- Perimeter = sum of the lengths of all three sides

Circle (Circumference):

- Circumference = 2 × π × radius or π × diameter

Sample Problems Using Measurement Formulas

Here are some example problems that illustrate the use of various measurement formulas, along with step-by-step explanations:

Problem 1: Distance Between Two Points

Problem: Calculate the distance between the points (3, 4) and (7, 1).

Solution:

1. Use the distance formula: Distance = sqrt((x2 - x1)^2 + (y2 - y1)^2)
2. Substitute the coordinates: Distance = sqrt((7 - 3)^2 + (1 - 4)^2)
3. Calculate the differences: Distance = sqrt(4^2 + (-3)^2)
4. Square the differences: Distance = sqrt(16 + 9)
5. Add the squares: Distance = sqrt(25)
6. Take the square root: Distance = 5

Answer: The distance between the points is 5 units.

Problem 2: Area of a Triangle

Problem: Find the area of a triangle with a base of 10 units and a height of 5 units.

Solution:

1. Use the area formula for a triangle: Area = 1/2 × base × height
2. Substitute the values: Area = 1/2 × 10 × 5
3. Multiply: Area = 1/2 × 50
4. Simplify: Area = 25

Answer: The area of the triangle is 25 square units.

Problem 3: Volume of a Cylinder

Problem: Calculate the volume of a cylinder with a radius of 3 units and a height of 7 units.

Solution:

1. Use the volume formula for a cylinder: Volume = $\pi \times$ radius^2 $\times$ height
2. Substitute the values: Volume = $\pi \times 3^2 \times 7$
3. Square the radius: Volume = $\pi \times 9 \times 7$
4. Multiply: Volume = $\pi \times 63$
5. Use $\pi \approx 3.14$ for calculation: Volume $\approx 3.14 \times 63$
6. Calculate: Volume ≈ 197.82

Answer: The volume of the cylinder is approximately 197.82 cubic units.

Problem 4: Perimeter of a Rectangle

Problem: Find the perimeter of a rectangle with a length of 8 units and a width of 5 units.

Solution:

1. Use the perimeter formula for a rectangle: Perimeter = 2 $\times$ (length + width)
2. Substitute the values: Perimeter = 2 $\times$ (8 + 5)
3. Add the length and width: Perimeter = 2 $\times$ 13
4. Multiply: Perimeter = 26

Answer: The perimeter of the rectangle is 26 units.

Problem 5: Area of a Circle

Problem: Calculate the area of a circle with a radius of 4 units.

Solution:

1. Use the area formula for a circle: Area = $\pi \times$ radius^2
2. Substitute the radius: Area = $\pi \times 4^2$
3. Square the radius: Area = $\pi \times 16$
4. Use $\pi \approx 3.14$ for calculation: Area $\approx 3.14 \times 16$
5. Calculate: Area ≈ 50.24

Answer: The area of the circle is approximately 50.24 square units.

Problem 6: Sum of Interior Angles of a Polygon

Problem: Determine the sum of the interior angles of a hexagon (6 sides).

Solution:

1. Use the formula for the sum of interior angles: Sum of interior angles = (n - 2) × 180 degrees
2. Substitute the number of sides (n = 6): Sum of interior angles = (6 - 2) × 180
3. Calculate: Sum of interior angles = 4 × 180
4. Multiply: Sum of interior angles = 720

Answer: The sum of the interior angles of a hexagon is 720 degrees.

These problems illustrate how to use various measurement formulas to solve real-world scenarios, providing clear steps for each calculation.

Complex Measurement Problems

Here are some complex problems involving measurement concepts, along with step-by-step explanations:

Problem 1: Volume and Surface Area of a Cone

Problem: Calculate the volume and surface area of a cone with a radius of 4 units and a height of 9 units.

Solution for Volume:

1. Use the volume formula for a cone: Volume = $(1/3) \times \pi \times radius^2 \times height$
2. Substitute the values: Volume = $(1/3) \times \pi \times 4^2 \times 9$
3. Square the radius: Volume = $(1/3) \times \pi \times 16 \times 9$
4. Multiply: Volume = $(1/3) \times \pi \times 144$
5. Simplify: Volume = 48π
6. Use $\pi \approx 3.14$ for calculation: Volume ≈ 48 × 3.14
7. Calculate: Volume ≈ 150.72

Solution for Surface Area:

1. Use the surface area formula for a cone: Surface Area = $\pi \times radius \times (radius + slant\ height)$
2. First, calculate the slant height using the Pythagorean theorem: Slant height = $sqrt(radius^2 + height^2)$
3. Substitute the values: Slant height = $sqrt(4^2 + 9^2)$
4. Calculate: Slant height = $sqrt(16 + 81)$ = $sqrt(97)$ ≈ 9.8
5. Use the surface area formula: Surface Area = $\pi \times 4 \times (4 + 9.8)$
6. Simplify: Surface Area = $\pi \times 4 \times 13.8$
7. Use $\pi \approx 3.14$ for calculation: Surface Area ≈ 3.14 × 4 × 13.8

8. Calculate: Surface Area ≈ 173.87

Answer: The volume of the cone is approximately 150.72 cubic units, and the surface area is approximately 173.87 square units.

Problem 2: Area of an Irregular Polygon

Problem: Find the area of an irregular polygon with vertices at $(1, 2)$, $(4, 3)$, $(5, 7)$, $(2, 6)$, and $(0, 4)$.

Solution:

1. Use the Shoelace formula for the area of a polygon: Area = $1/2 \times | \Sigma(x_i y_{i+1} - x_{i+1} y_i) |$
2. List the coordinates cyclically: $(1, 2)$, $(4, 3)$, $(5, 7)$, $(2, 6)$, $(0, 4)$, $(1, 2)$
3. Calculate the products of the coordinates:
   - $(1\cdot3 + 4\cdot7 + 5\cdot6 + 2\cdot4 + 0\cdot2) - (2\cdot4 + 3\cdot5 + 7\cdot2 + 6\cdot0 + 4\cdot1)$
   - $= (3 + 28 + 30 + 8 + 0) - (8 + 15 + 14 + 0 + 4)$
   - $= 69 - 41$
   - $= 28$
4. Apply the formula: Area = $1/2 \times |28| = 14$

Answer: The area of the irregular polygon is 14 square units.

Problem 3: Distance and Midpoint Between Two Points in 3D Space

Problem: Calculate the distance and the midpoint between the points $(2, -1, 3)$ and $(6, 2, -5)$ in 3D space.

Solution for Distance:

1. Use the distance formula for 3D space: Distance = $\sqrt{(x_2 - x_1)^2 + (y_2 - y_1)^2 + (z_2 - z_1)^2}$
2. Substitute the coordinates: Distance = $\sqrt{(6 - 2)^2 + (2 - (-1))^2 + (-5 - 3)^2}$
3. Calculate the differences: Distance = $\sqrt{4^2 + 3^2 + (-8)^2}$
4. Square the differences: Distance = $\sqrt{16 + 9 + 64}$
5. Add the squares: Distance = $\sqrt{89}$
6. Simplify: Distance ≈ 9.43

Solution for Midpoint:

1. Use the midpoint formula for 3D space: Midpoint = $((x_1 + x_2)/2, (y_1 + y_2)/2, (z_1 + z_2)/2)$
2. Substitute the coordinates: Midpoint = $((2 + 6)/2, (-1 + 2)/2, (3 - 5)/2)$
3. Calculate the sums: Midpoint = $(8/2, 1/2, -2/2)$
4. Simplify: Midpoint = $(4, 0.5, -1)$

Answer: The distance between the points is approximately 9.43 units, and the midpoint is $(4, 0.5, -1)$.

PART V
SCIENCE

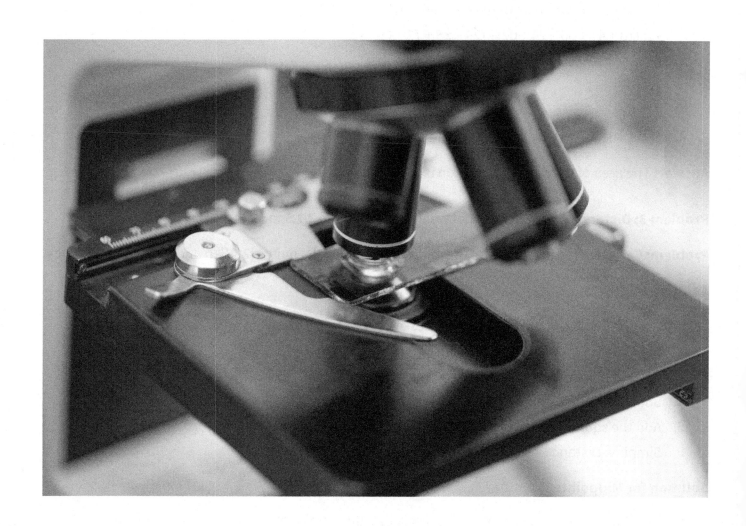

SCIENTIFIC REASONING SKILLS

Scientific reasoning is an essential skill for the GED Science Test. It involves the ability to think critically about scientific concepts and data. This section of the test measures your understanding of the scientific method, the design of experiments, and the interpretation of data and results.

The Scientific Method

- **Observation**: Everything in science starts with observation. It's about noticing the world around you and asking questions about why things are the way they are.
- **Hypothesis**: After observations, scientists propose a hypothesis—a tentative explanation that can be tested through experiments.

Critical Thinking in Science

- **Questioning**: Critical thinking begins with asking the right questions. It's about being curious and skeptical, not taking things at face value.
- **Analysis**: It involves breaking down complex information into understandable parts and examining the evidence critically.

Data Interpretation

Interpreting data is a key component of scientific reasoning. The GED Science Test will often present you with graphs, tables, and charts, requiring you to extract and analyze information.

Reading Graphs and Tables

- **Identifying Trends**: Look for patterns in the data. Is there an upward or downward trend? What does this tell you about the relationship between variables?
- **Comparing Data Points**: It's not just about what the data shows; it's also about what it doesn't show. Are there outliers? What could they indicate?

Evaluating Data

- **Reliability**: Consider the source of the data. Is it from a reputable, peer-reviewed scientific journal or a less reliable source?
- **Relevance**: Does the data directly support the hypothesis, or is it tangential? Always consider the context of the data.

Understanding Scientific Experiments

The GED Science Test assesses your ability to comprehend the design and outcomes of scientific experiments. This includes understanding variables, controls, and the experimental process.

Experimental Design

A well-designed experiment is the foundation of reliable scientific data. Key components include a clear hypothesis, independent and dependent variables, controls, and a sufficient sample size. Recognizing these elements is important for analyzing any experiment.

In experimental design, the following are worth noting:

- **Variables**: Identify the independent and dependent variables. The independent variable is what you change, and the dependent variable is what you measure.
- **Controls**: These are the constants in an experiment. They help ensure that the test results are due to the independent variable, not some other factor.

Interpreting Experimental Results

Once an experiment is conducted, the results must be analyzed. This involves looking at the data collected, determining whether it supports the hypothesis, and considering the implications of the findings.

- **Data Collection**: Look at how the data was collected. Was the methodology sound? Were there any biases that could have affected the results?
- **Conclusions**: Can you draw a direct line from the data to the conclusion? Are the results statistically significant?

The Role of Theories and Laws

Scientific theories and laws are the cornerstones of scientific understanding. They are based on evidence and can predict the outcome of future experiments.

Scientific Theories

A scientific theory is a well-substantiated explanation of some aspect of the natural world. It's based on a body of evidence and can change as new evidence emerges. Understanding theories is crucial for scientific reasoning.

Please, note the following:

- **Evidence-Based**: Theories are not guesses. They are comprehensive explanations backed by a significant amount of evidence.
- **Evolving**: As new evidence comes to light, theories can be adapted or even replaced. Science is always a work in progress.

Scientific Laws

A scientific law is a statement based on repeated experimental observations that describe some aspect of the world. Laws predict the results of certain initial conditions and are often expressed mathematically.

- **Descriptive**: Laws describe natural phenomena. They tell us what happens under certain conditions, often expressed mathematically.
- **Predictive**: Laws allow us to predict what will happen in a given situation, as long as the conditions are the same.

Problem-Solving with Science

Scientific reasoning is a powerful tool for problem-solving. It allows you to approach complex issues methodically, using evidence to inform decisions and solutions.

- **Methodical Approach**: Use the scientific method to approach problems systematically. Start with a question and follow through to the conclusion.
- **Evidence-Based Decisions**: Make decisions based on evidence, not assumptions. This is the heart of scientific reasoning.

Science in Everyday Life

Science is not confined to the laboratory. It's all around us, from the technology we use to the natural processes that shape our environment. Understanding science helps you make informed decisions in everyday life.

- **Informed Decisions**: Whether it's about health, technology, or the environment, understanding science helps you make better decisions.
- **Lifelong Learning**: Science is constantly evolving. Stay curious and keep learning. It's a lifelong journey.

LIFE SCIENCE FUNDAMENTALS

The life sciences encompass a broad array of fields that study living organisms, their life processes, and their interactions with each other and their environments. In the GED's science section, understanding the basics of life science is essential for answering questions related to biology and the life sciences. Here are some fundamental concepts that are typically covered. Use these as stepping stones into further expanded research:

Cell Biology

Cell biology is the study of the structural and functional units of life: cells. This section covers the differences between cell types, the structures within cells, and the vital processes they perform.

Cell Structure and Function: Cells are the fundamental units of life. There are two primary types of cells: prokaryotic and eukaryotic.

- **Prokaryotic Cells:** These cells do not have a nucleus. Bacteria are the most common examples. They have a simple structure with DNA floating freely within the cell.
- **Eukaryotic Cells:** These cells have a nucleus that contains their DNA. They are more complex and are found in plants, animals, fungi, and protists.

Key components of eukaryotic cells include:

- **Cell Membrane:** A protective barrier that controls what enters and exits the cell.
- **Cytoplasm:** The jelly-like substance within the cell where organelles are suspended.
- **Nucleus:** Contains genetic material (DNA) and controls cell activities.
- **Mitochondria:** Known as the powerhouse of the cell, they generate energy through cellular respiration.
- **Ribosomes:** Synthesize proteins by following instructions from the DNA.
- **Chloroplasts:** Found in plant cells, these organelles conduct photosynthesis by converting sunlight into chemical energy.
- **Endoplasmic Reticulum (ER):** Involved in protein and lipid synthesis; rough ER has ribosomes, while smooth ER does not.
- **Golgi Apparatus:** Modifies, sorts, and packages proteins for secretion or use within the cell.

Cell Functions:

- **Metabolism:** All chemical reactions that occur within a cell, including those that provide energy and build cell components.
- **Energy Conversion:** Cells convert nutrients into usable energy, primarily in the form of ATP, through processes like cellular respiration and photosynthesis.

- **Reproduction:** Cells reproduce through processes such as mitosis (for growth and repair) and meiosis (for producing gametes in sexually reproducing organisms).

Genetics and Heredity

Genetics and heredity explore how traits are passed from parents to offspring through genes. This section delves into the structure and function of DNA, Mendelian genetics, and the genetic variations that contribute to diversity among organisms.

DNA and Genes:

- **DNA (Deoxyribonucleic Acid):** The molecule that carries genetic instructions for the development, functioning, growth, and reproduction of all known living organisms.
- **Genes:** Segments of DNA that code for proteins, which carry out all functions in a cell.

Mendelian Genetics:

- **Gregor Mendel:** The father of modern genetics, Mendel discovered the basic principles of heredity through experiments with pea plants.
- **Dominant and Recessive Traits:** Traits are determined by alleles. Dominant alleles mask the expression of recessive alleles.
- **Genotype vs. Phenotype:** Genotype refers to the genetic makeup of an organism, while phenotype refers to the observable traits.
- **Punnett Squares:** Tools used to predict the probability of inheriting particular traits.

Genetic Variation:

- **Mutations:** Changes in DNA sequence that can lead to genetic diversity.
- **Sexual Reproduction:** Combines genetic material from two parents, leading to offspring with genetic variation.

Evolution and Natural Selection

Evolution and natural selection explain how species change over time and adapt to their environments. This section covers the mechanisms of evolution, including natural selection, and provides evidence supporting evolutionary theory.

Evolution:

- **Theory of Evolution:** Proposes that species change over time through processes such as mutation, natural selection, and genetic drift.
- **Fossil Record:** Provides evidence of past life forms and their changes over time.

Natural Selection:

- **Charles Darwin:** Proposed that organisms better adapted to their environment tend to survive and reproduce, passing advantageous traits to their offspring.
- **Survival of the Fittest:** The concept that individuals with favorable traits are more likely to survive and reproduce.
- **Adaptation:** Traits that enhance an organism's ability to survive and reproduce in a particular environment.

Ecology

Ecology examines how organisms interact with each other and their environments. This section explores the structure and dynamics of ecosystems, energy flow through food webs, and the impact of human activities on natural systems.

Ecosystems:

- **Definition:** Communities of living organisms interacting with their physical environment.
- **Components:** Include biotic factors (living things like plants, animals, and microorganisms) and abiotic factors (non-living things like sunlight, water, and soil).

Food Webs:

- **Producers:** Organisms that make their own food (e.g., plants through photosynthesis).
- **Consumers:** Organisms that eat other organisms (e.g., herbivores, carnivores, omnivores).
- **Decomposers:** Organisms that break down dead material, returning nutrients to the environment (e.g., fungi and bacteria).

Energy Flow:

- **Trophic Levels:** Different levels in a food web, including producers, primary consumers, secondary consumers, and tertiary consumers.
- **Energy Transfer:** Only about 10% of energy is transferred from one trophic level to the next, with the rest lost as heat.

Human Impact:

- **Deforestation:** The removal of trees, which can lead to habitat loss and decreased biodiversity.
- **Pollution:** Contaminants that can harm ecosystems and human health.
- **Climate Change:** Changes in global or regional climate patterns, primarily due to increased levels of atmospheric carbon dioxide from the use of fossil fuels.

Human Biology

Human biology focuses on the study of the human body and its systems. This section covers the major systems that maintain homeostasis and support life, as well as the concept of homeostasis itself.

Major Systems of the Human Body:

- **Circulatory System:** Includes the heart and blood vessels; responsible for transporting blood, nutrients, oxygen, and waste products throughout the body.
- **Respiratory System:** Includes the lungs; responsible for gas exchange, taking in oxygen and expelling carbon dioxide.
- **Digestive System:** Includes the stomach and intestines; breaks down food into nutrients that can be absorbed into the bloodstream.
- **Nervous System:** Includes the brain, spinal cord, and nerves; controls body functions and responses to stimuli.
- **Musculoskeletal System:** Includes bones and muscles; provides structure, support, and movement.

Homeostasis:

- **Definition:** The process by which the body maintains a stable internal environment despite changes in external conditions.
- **Examples:** Regulation of body temperature, blood sugar levels, and pH balance.

Biotechnology

Biotechnology involves using living organisms or their components to develop products and technologies that improve human life and the health of the planet. This section explores the applications and advances made possible by biotechnology.

Genetic Engineering:

- **Definition:** The direct manipulation of an organism's genes using biotechnology.
- **Applications:** Includes the production of insulin, development of genetically modified crops, and gene therapy.

Medical Advances:

- **Vaccines:** Biological preparations that provide immunity to specific diseases.
- **Antibiotics:** Drugs used to treat bacterial infections.

- **Stem Cell Research:** Studying undifferentiated cells that have the potential to develop into different cell types.

INTRODUCTION TO PHYSICAL SCIENCE

The physical sciences encompass a range of fields that study non-living systems, including chemistry, physics, and Earth science. In the context of the GED science section, understanding the basics of physical science is crucial for answering questions related to these disciplines. Here are some fundamental concepts that are typically covered. As with the life sciences section, these are only meant to introduce the concepts to the reader and will warrant further research:

Matter and Its Properties

Matter is anything that has mass and occupies space. This section covers the different states of matter, the properties of matter, and how matter interacts through chemical and physical changes.

States of Matter:

- **Solids:** Have a fixed shape and volume. The particles are closely packed together and vibrate in place.
- **Liquids:** Have a definite volume but take the shape of their container. The particles are close together but can move past one another.
- **Gases:** Have neither a fixed shape nor a fixed volume. The particles are far apart and move freely.
- **Plasma:** An ionized state of matter similar to gas but with free electrons, found in stars and neon lights.

Properties of Matter:

- **Physical Properties:** Characteristics that can be observed without changing the substance's chemical identity, such as color, density, and melting point.
- **Chemical Properties:** Characteristics that describe a substance's ability to change into different substances, such as flammability and reactivity.

Chemical vs. Physical Changes:

- **Physical Changes:** Changes in the form of matter but not its chemical identity, such as melting, freezing, and dissolving.

- **Chemical Changes:** Changes that result in the formation of new substances with different properties, such as rusting and combustion.

Atomic Structure

Atoms are the basic units of matter, consisting of protons, neutrons, and electrons. This section explores the structure of atoms, the periodic table, and the concepts of isotopes and ions.

Atomic Structure:

- **Nucleus:** The center of the atom, containing protons (positively charged) and neutrons (neutral).
- **Electrons:** Negatively charged particles that orbit the nucleus in electron shells.

The Periodic Table:

- **Elements:** Pure substances consisting of only one type of atom, represented on the periodic table.
- **Groups and Periods:** The periodic table is organized into rows (periods) and columns (groups) that classify elements by their chemical properties.
- **Metals, Nonmetals, and Metalloids:** Elements are categorized based on their physical and chemical properties.

Isotopes and Ions:

Isotopes: Atoms of the same element with different numbers of neutrons.

Ions: Atoms that have gained or lost electrons, resulting in a net charge.

Chemical Reactions

Chemical reactions involve the transformation of reactants into products. This section covers the types of chemical reactions, the law of conservation of mass, and the basics of balancing chemical equations.

Types of Chemical Reactions:

- **Synthesis Reactions:** Two or more simple substances combine to form a more complex substance ($A + B \rightarrow AB$).
- **Decomposition Reactions:** A complex substance breaks down into two or more simpler substances ($AB \rightarrow A + B$).
- **Single Replacement Reactions:** One element replaces another in a compound ($A + BC \rightarrow AC + B$).

- **Double Replacement Reactions:** Two compounds exchange elements or groups of elements (AB + CD → AD + CB).

Law of Conservation of Mass:

- **Definition:** In a chemical reaction, mass is neither created nor destroyed; the mass of the reactants equals the mass of the products.

Balancing Chemical Equations:

- **Importance:** Ensures that the same number of each type of atom is present on both sides of the equation.
- **Steps:** Identify reactants and products, count atoms of each element, and adjust coefficients to balance the atoms.

Forces and Motion

Forces and motion are fundamental concepts in physics that describe how objects move and interact. This section explains Newton's laws of motion, the concepts of force and work, and the principles of momentum and energy.

Newton's Laws of Motion:

- **First Law (Inertia):** An object at rest stays at rest, and an object in motion stays in motion unless acted upon by an external force.
- **Second Law (F=ma):** The acceleration of an object is directly proportional to the net force acting on it and inversely proportional to its mass.
- **Third Law (Action and Reaction):** For every action, there is an equal and opposite reaction.

Force and Work:

- **Force:** A push or pull acting upon an object resulting from its interaction with another object.
- **Work:** The transfer of energy that occurs when a force makes an object move (Work = Force × Distance).

Momentum and Energy:

- **Momentum:** The product of an object's mass and velocity ($p = mv$).
- **Kinetic Energy:** The energy an object has due to its motion ($KE = 1/2\ mv^2$).
- **Potential Energy:** The stored energy an object has due to its position or state (e.g., gravitational potential energy).

Energy and Thermodynamics

Energy exists in various forms and is subject to the laws of thermodynamics. This section covers the different types of energy, the principles of energy transfer, and the laws that govern thermodynamic processes.

Types of Energy:

- **Kinetic Energy:** Energy of motion.
- **Potential Energy:** Stored energy.
- **Thermal Energy:** Energy related to the temperature of an object.
- **Chemical Energy:** Energy stored in chemical bonds.
- **Electrical Energy:** Energy from electric currents.
- **Nuclear Energy:** Energy stored in the nucleus of an atom.

Energy Transfer:

- **Conduction:** Transfer of heat through direct contact.
- **Convection:** Transfer of heat through fluid movement.
- **Radiation:** Transfer of energy through electromagnetic waves.

Laws of Thermodynamics:

- **First Law (Conservation of Energy):** Energy cannot be created or destroyed, only transformed from one form to another.
- **Second Law (Entropy):** In any energy transfer, some energy becomes unavailable to do work, increasing the disorder (entropy) of the system.
- **Third Law:** As temperature approaches absolute zero, the entropy of a system approaches a constant minimum.

Waves and Electromagnetic Spectrum

Waves are disturbances that transfer energy from one place to another. This section covers the properties of waves, the electromagnetic spectrum, and the behavior of light and sound waves.

Properties of Waves:

- **Wavelength:** The distance between successive crests or troughs.
- **Frequency:** The number of waves that pass a point in a given time period.
- **Amplitude:** The height of the wave, related to its energy.
- **Speed:** The distance a wave travels in a given time period.

Electromagnetic Spectrum:

- **Definition:** The range of all types of electromagnetic radiation.
- **Types:** Includes radio waves, microwaves, infrared, visible light, ultraviolet, X-rays, and gamma rays.
- **Applications:** Each type of radiation has different uses, from communication (radio waves) to medical imaging (X-rays).

Behavior of Light and Sound:

- **Reflection:** The bouncing of waves off a surface.
- **Refraction:** The bending of waves as they pass from one medium to another.
- **Diffraction:** The spreading of waves around obstacles.
- **Interference:** The interaction of waves that meet, creating patterns of reinforcement or cancellation.

These basics provide a foundation for exploring more complex topics and for appreciating the principles that govern the physical world.

EARTH AND SPACE SCIENCE CONCEPTS

Earth and space science explores the processes that shape our planet and the universe beyond. Here are some fundamental topics covered in this area of the Science section:

Earth's Structure and Systems

Understanding Earth's structure and the systems that operate within it is crucial for comprehending geological and environmental processes. This section covers the composition of Earth, the rock cycle, plate tectonics, and the various spheres that interact to support life.

Earth's Layers:

- **Crust:** The thin, outermost layer where we live, composed of solid rocks and minerals.
- **Mantle:** The thick, middle layer made of semi-solid rock that flows slowly.
- **Core:** Composed of an outer liquid layer and a solid inner layer, primarily made of iron and nickel.

Rock Cycle:

- **Igneous Rocks:** Formed from the cooling and solidification of magma or lava.
- **Sedimentary Rocks:** Created from the compaction and cementation of sediments.
- **Metamorphic Rocks:** Formed when existing rocks are subjected to heat and pressure, causing them to change.

Plate Tectonics:

- **Theory:** Explains the movement of Earth's lithospheric plates and the activity at their boundaries.
- **Boundaries:** Include divergent (plates move apart), convergent (plates move together), and transform (plates slide past each other).

Earth's Spheres:

- **Geosphere:** The solid part of Earth, including rocks and landforms.
- **Hydrosphere:** All of Earth's water, including oceans, lakes, rivers, and glaciers.
- **Atmosphere:** The layer of gases surrounding Earth.
- **Biosphere:** All living organisms and the ecosystems they inhabit.

Weather and Climate

Weather and climate study atmospheric conditions and long-term weather patterns. This section explores the factors that influence weather, the tools used to measure atmospheric conditions, and the differences between weather and climate.

Weather:

- **Definition:** The state of the atmosphere at a specific place and time, including temperature, humidity, precipitation, and wind.
- **Measurement Tools:** Thermometers (temperature), barometers (air pressure), anemometers (wind speed), and hygrometers (humidity).

Climate:

- **Definition:** The average weather conditions in an area over a long period.
- **Factors:** Include latitude, elevation, proximity to water bodies, and ocean currents.

Atmospheric Circulation:

- **Wind Patterns:** Created by the uneven heating of Earth's surface, leading to high and low-pressure systems.
- **Jet Streams:** High-altitude, fast-moving air currents that influence weather patterns.

Severe Weather:

- **Types:** Include hurricanes, tornadoes, thunderstorms, and blizzards.
- **Formation:** Understanding how these severe weather events develop and their impact on the environment and human activity.

Astronomy and the Universe

Astronomy is the study of celestial objects and the universe as a whole. This section covers the solar system, the lifecycle of stars, galaxies, and the fundamental principles that govern the cosmos.

The Solar System:

- **Sun:** The star at the center of our solar system, providing the energy necessary for life on Earth.
- **Planets:** Eight planets orbit the sun, divided into terrestrial (rocky) and gas giants.
- **Moons, Asteroids, and Comets:** Smaller celestial bodies that orbit the sun or planets.

Stars and Galaxies:

- **Lifecycle of Stars:** Stars form from clouds of gas and dust, go through various stages (main sequence, red giant, white dwarf, etc.), and end as black holes, neutron stars, or supernovae.
- **Galaxies:** Massive systems of stars, gas, and dust held together by gravity. Our solar system is part of the Milky Way galaxy.

The Big Bang Theory:

- **Theory:** The prevailing explanation for the origin of the universe, suggesting it began as a singularity approximately 13.8 billion years ago and has been expanding ever since.

Telescopes and Space Exploration:

- **Telescopes:** Instruments that collect and magnify light from distant objects, allowing us to observe celestial bodies.
- **Space Missions:** Human and robotic missions that have explored space, providing valuable data about our solar system and beyond.

Environmental Science

Environmental science examines the interactions between the natural world and human activities. This section discusses ecosystems, natural resources, pollution, and the impact of human actions on the environment.

Ecosystems:

- **Components:** Biotic (living) and abiotic (non-living) elements that interact within an ecosystem.
- **Biodiversity:** The variety of life within an ecosystem, important for resilience and stability.

Natural Resources:

- **Renewable Resources:** Resources that can be replenished naturally, such as solar energy, wind, and biomass.
- **Non-Renewable Resources:** Resources that are finite and will eventually be depleted, such as fossil fuels and minerals.

Pollution:

- **Types:** Include air, water, soil, and noise pollution.
- **Sources:** Industrial processes, agricultural activities, waste disposal, and transportation.

Human Impact:

- **Climate Change:** The alteration of Earth's climate due to increased levels of greenhouse gases from human activities.
- **Conservation Efforts:** Strategies to protect natural habitats, preserve biodiversity, and promote sustainable resource use.

By understanding these fundamental concepts of Earth and space science, you will be well-prepared to tackle questions related to geology, meteorology, astronomy, and environmental science on the GED science section. These basics provide a foundation for exploring more complex topics and for appreciating the processes that shape our planet and the universe.

PART VI
SOCIAL STUDIES

Social studies encompass a broad array of subjects that delve into the human experience, including history, government, economics, geography, and civics. Since the GED is primarily meant for North American students, its social studies section also narrows in on that part of the world. This section of the *GED Study Guide* focuses on U.S. history and government, exploring the foundational principles, key events, and political institutions that have shaped the United States.

At the end of this Part, you'll find a list of world history events that you should explore to be well-prepared for the GED's Social Studies section.

U.S. HISTORY AND GOVERNMENT

U.S. history is woven with the threads of triumphs, struggles, and transformations that have defined the American experience. From the earliest colonial settlements to the present day, understanding the trajectory of U.S. history is essential for grasping the complexities of the nation's identity and its place in the world.

The journey of Colonial America marks the genesis of the American story, as European explorers ventured across the Atlantic in search of new opportunities and encounters. The colonial period witnessed the clash of cultures, the forging of new societies, and the laying of foundations upon which the United States would be built. From the first tentative footsteps on the shores of the New World to the establishment of thriving colonies, Colonial America set the stage for the epic saga of American history.

Colonial America

The colonial period in American history marks the earliest European settlements in the New World, beginning with the arrival of Spanish explorers in the 16th century and continuing with the establishment of British colonies along the eastern seaboard. This era was characterized by exploration, exploitation, and the interplay of diverse cultures as Europeans encountered indigenous peoples and established footholds in the Americas.

As European powers vied for dominance and resources in the New World, colonies emerged as outposts of empire, serving as centers of trade, agriculture, and settlement. The Jamestown settlement in Virginia, founded in 1607, and the Plymouth Colony in Massachusetts, established by the Pilgrims in 1620, were among the earliest permanent English settlements, laying the groundwork for the expansion of British influence in North America.

The colonial period was marked by a complex interplay of economic, social, and political forces, including the growth of slavery, the emergence of representative government, and the spread of religious diversity. These developments laid the foundation for the American Revolution and the birth of a new nation founded on the principles of liberty, democracy, and equality.

Key Themes:

- **Religious Freedom:** Many settlers came to America seeking religious freedom and the opportunity to worship according to their beliefs, leading to the founding of colonies such as Massachusetts and Rhode Island.
- **Economic Opportunity:** Colonists also sought economic opportunities in America, engaging in activities such as agriculture, trade, and manufacturing to build prosperous communities.

- **Indigenous Relations:** The arrival of Europeans had profound impacts on indigenous peoples, leading to conflicts, alliances, and cultural exchanges that shaped the course of American history.

The American Revolution

The American Revolution, fought from 1775 to 1783, was a pivotal event in U.S. history that resulted in the thirteen colonies gaining independence from British rule.

Key Events:

- Battles of Lexington and Concord: The first military engagements of the Revolutionary War, marking the beginning of armed conflict between colonial militias and British forces.
- Declaration of Independence: The adoption of the Declaration of Independence on July 4, 1776, proclaiming the colonies' independence and asserting the principles of liberty and self-governance.
- Victory at Yorktown: The decisive victory of American and French forces over the British at Yorktown, Virginia, in 1781, leading to the British surrender and the end of major hostilities.

The Founding of the Republic

The founding of the United States as a constitutional republic was a pivotal moment in history, characterized by the drafting and ratification of the U.S. Constitution in 1787. This monumental document established the framework for the federal government and laid the groundwork for the nation's political system, ensuring a balance of power and protecting the rights and liberties of its citizens.

Key Figures in the Founding Era

The Founding Fathers played instrumental roles in shaping the destiny of the young nation, each contributing their unique talents, perspectives, and leadership to the cause of American independence and self-governance.

George Washington

George Washington, revered as the "Father of His Country," was not only the first President of the United States but also a key leader during the Revolutionary War. His steadfast leadership, integrity, and dedication to the cause of liberty earned him the respect and admiration of his fellow citizens. As president, Washington presided over the Constitutional Convention in Philadelphia in 1787, where he provided invaluable guidance and wisdom in crafting the framework of the new government. His presidency set important precedents for presidential authority, including the peaceful transfer of power and the principle of civilian control over the military.

James Madison

James Madison, often hailed as the "Father of the Constitution," played a central role in drafting the U.S. Constitution and advocating for its ratification. His deep understanding of political theory and his commitment to republican principles were instrumental in shaping the structure and functions of the federal government.

Madison's contributions to the Federalist Papers, a series of essays written to promote ratification of the Constitution, helped sway public opinion and garner support for the new government. As the primary author of the Bill of Rights, Madison also ensured the inclusion of essential protections for individual liberties, such as freedom of speech, religion, and due process of law.

Alexander Hamilton

Alexander Hamilton, a brilliant statesman and visionary thinker, made significant contributions to the founding of the republic, particularly in the realm of economic policy and constitutional interpretation. As the first Secretary of the Treasury, Hamilton played a key role in shaping the nation's financial system, advocating for the establishment of a national bank, a system of tariffs and taxes, and the assumption of state debts. His seminal work, *The Federalist Papers*, co-authored with James Madison and John Jay, provided a comprehensive defense of the Constitution and outlined the rationale for a strong federal government. Hamilton's legacy continues to resonate in the realms of finance, law, and governance, as his ideas and principles remain central to debates over the role of government and the nature of constitutional authority.

Challenges and Compromises

The process of drafting and ratifying the U.S. Constitution was not without its challenges and compromises. As delegates gathered in Philadelphia in 1787, they faced daunting tasks and contentious debates over issues such as representation, federalism, and the balance of power between the states and the federal government.

Representation and Federalism

One of the key debates at the Constitutional Convention revolved around the issue of representation in the national legislature. Larger states, such as Virginia and Pennsylvania, argued for representation based on population, while smaller states, such as New Jersey and Delaware, advocated for equal representation for all states. The Great Compromise, proposed by Roger Sherman of Connecticut, resolved this dispute by creating a bicameral legislature consisting of the House of Representatives, where representation would be based on population, and the Senate, where each state would have equal representation.

Checks and Balances

The framers of the Constitution sought to establish a system of checks and balances to prevent any one branch of government from becoming too powerful. The separation of powers between the legislative, executive, and judicial branches, as outlined in the Constitution, was designed to ensure that each branch would have distinct powers and responsibilities, while also providing mechanisms for oversight and accountability. The system of checks and balances allows each branch to limit the powers of the other branches, thereby safeguarding against tyranny and abuse of power.

Ratification and the Bill of Rights

After the Constitution was drafted, it faced the arduous task of ratification by the states. Supporters of the Constitution, known as Federalists, argued for its adoption, while opponents, known as Anti-Federalists, raised concerns about the potential for centralized power and the lack of explicit protections for individual rights. In order to secure ratification, the Federalists agreed to add a series of amendments to the Constitution known as the Bill of Rights. These amendments, which were designed to safeguard individual liberties and limit the power of the federal government, proved crucial in winning over skeptics and ensuring the ultimate success of the Constitution.

Legacy of the Founding Era

The legacy of the founding era continues to shape American politics, law, and society to this day. The principles and ideals embodied in the Constitution - including democracy, equality, and the rule of law - remain guiding principles for the nation, providing a foundation for the ongoing struggle to form a more perfect union.

As citizens of the United States, it is essential to understand and appreciate the achievements of the founding era, as well as the challenges and compromises that shaped the nation's founding document.

Manifest Destiny and Westward Expansion

Manifest Destiny was the belief that it was America's destiny to expand across the North American continent, driven by a sense of cultural superiority and economic opportunity.

Key Concepts:

- **Louisiana Purchase:** President Thomas Jefferson's acquisition of the Louisiana Territory from France in 1803, doubling the size of the United States and opening up vast new lands for settlement.

- **Oregon Trail:** A historic east-west wagon route that connected the Missouri River to Oregon, allowing thousands of pioneers to migrate westward in search of land and opportunity.
- **Mexican-American War**: A conflict fought from 1846 to 1848 between the United States and Mexico, resulting in the annexation of Texas and the cession of California, New Mexico, and other territories to the United States.

The Civil War and Reconstruction

The Civil War, spanning from 1861 to 1865, stands as a watershed moment in American history, tearing the nation apart and ultimately reshaping its future. This conflict, waged primarily over issues of slavery and states' rights, tested the resilience of the young republic and exacted a heavy toll in lives lost and communities ravaged.

Key Events of the Civil War

At the heart of the Civil War were pivotal events that shifted the course of the conflict and determined its outcome. The Battle of Gettysburg, fought in July 1863 on the fields of Pennsylvania, stands as a defining moment in the war, marking a turning point in favor of the Union forces. This epic clash resulted in a decisive Union victory and dealt a severe blow to the Confederate army, effectively halting their advance into Northern territory.

President Abraham Lincoln's Emancipation Proclamation, issued in 1863, represented a bold step towards the abolition of slavery in the United States. While its immediate impact was limited, as it only applied to Confederate-held territory, the proclamation signaled a significant shift in the war's aims and galvanized support for the Union cause. By declaring all slaves in rebel states to be free, Lincoln sought to undermine the economic and social foundations of the Confederacy, while also appealing to the moral imperative of ending slavery.

Reconstruction Amendments

In the aftermath of the Civil War, the United States embarked on a period of Reconstruction aimed at rebuilding the shattered nation and addressing the legacy of slavery and racial inequality. Central to this effort were the Reconstruction Amendments - the 13th, 14th, and 15th Amendments to the Constitution - which sought to enshrine the principles of equality and citizenship for all Americans.

The 13th Amendment, ratified in 1865, abolished slavery throughout the United States, marking a historic milestone in the nation's journey towards freedom and justice. Building upon this foundation, the 14th Amendment, ratified in 1868, granted citizenship and equal protection under the law to all persons born or naturalized in the United States, regardless of race or previous condition of servitude.

This landmark amendment aimed to safeguard the rights of newly freed slaves and ensure their full participation in American society.

The 15th Amendment, ratified in 1870, further expanded the franchise by guaranteeing voting rights to African American men, prohibiting states from denying the right to vote based on race, color, or previous servitude. These Reconstruction Amendments represented a profound transformation in the nation's constitutional framework, affirming the principles of equality and democracy and laying the groundwork for a more inclusive and just society.

Industrialization and the Gilded Age

The late 19th century witnessed rapid industrialization and urbanization in the United States, transforming the nation's economy and society.

Key Developments:

- **Rise of Big Business:** The emergence of large corporations and trusts in industries such as oil, steel, and railroads, leading to increased consolidation of wealth and economic power.
- **Labor Unions:** The rise of labor unions and the labor movement, advocating for workers' rights, better wages, and improved working conditions in the face of exploitation and abuse by employers.
- **Social Reform Movements:** Progressive reformers sought to address social and economic injustices through legislation and activism, leading to reforms such as child labor laws, workplace safety regulations, and women's suffrage.

U.S. Government

The U.S. government is based on the principles of federalism, separation of powers, and checks and balances, as outlined in the Constitution. Understanding the structure, functions, and responsibilities of the federal government is essential for informed citizenship and effective participation in the democratic process.

The Three Branches of Government

The federal government is divided into three branches: the legislative, executive, and judicial branches, each with distinct powers and responsibilities.

Legislative Branch:

- Congress, consisting of the Senate and the House of Representatives, is responsible for making laws, levying taxes, and regulating interstate commerce.
- The Senate, with two senators from each state, provides equal representation for all states, while the House of Representatives, with representatives based on population, ensures proportional representation.

Executive Branch:

- The President, as the head of the executive branch, is responsible for enforcing laws, conducting foreign policy, and serving as Commander-in-Chief of the armed forces.
- The President's powers include the ability to veto legislation, appoint federal judges and executive officials, and issue executive orders to implement laws and policies.

Judicial Branch:

- The judicial branch, headed by the Supreme Court, interprets laws, resolves disputes, and ensures that the Constitution is upheld.
- The Supreme Court has the authority to review the constitutionality of laws and executive actions through the process of judicial review, as established in the landmark case Marbury v. Madison (1803).

The Constitution and Bill of Rights

The U.S. Constitution, ratified in 1788, is the supreme law of the land, establishing the framework for the federal government and guaranteeing fundamental rights and freedoms to American citizens.

Key Principles:

- **Federalism**: The division of powers between the federal government and state governments, with each level of government having its own sphere of authority.
- **Separation of Powers:** The allocation of distinct powers and functions to the legislative, executive, and judicial branches, preventing any one branch from gaining too much power.
- **Checks and Balances:** The system of checks and balances ensures that each branch of government can limit the powers of the other branches, maintaining a balance of power and preventing tyranny.

The Bill of Rights:

- The first ten amendments to the Constitution, collectively known as the Bill of Rights, protect individual liberties such as freedom of speech, religion, and the press, as well as due process and equal protection under the law.
- The Bill of Rights guarantees essential rights and freedoms to American citizens, ensuring that the government respects their civil liberties and constitutional rights.

Federalism and State Government

Federalism is the division of powers between the federal government and state governments, with each level of government having its own sphere of authority.

State Powers:

- State governments have powers reserved to them by the Tenth Amendment, such as regulating education, conducting elections, and maintaining public health and safety.
- States also have the authority to pass laws and policies that reflect the unique needs and priorities of their residents, allowing for flexibility and diversity in governance.

Citizenship and Civic Engagement

Citizenship entails both rights and responsibilities, including voting, serving on juries, paying taxes, and obeying laws.

Rights of Citizenship:

- Citizenship confers important rights and privileges, such as the right to vote in elections, the right to petition the government, and the right to due process of law.
- These rights are guaranteed by the Constitution and reflect the principles of democracy, equality, and individual liberty.

Responsibilities of Citizenship:

- Citizenship also comes with responsibilities, such as obeying laws, paying taxes, serving on juries, and defending the country in times of need.
- Civic engagement involves active participation in the democratic process, such as voting in elections, attending public meetings, and advocating for social and political change.

Overview of Key Eras to Study

1. Colonial America (1607-1776):

- **Key Events:** Founding of Jamestown, Pilgrims and Puritans, development of the Thirteen Colonies.
- **Important Figures:** John Smith, Pocahontas, William Penn, and Benjamin Franklin.
- **Themes:** Colonization, Native American relations, development of colonial governments, and economic activities.

2. The American Revolution (1775-1783):

- **Key Events:** Battles of Lexington and Concord, Declaration of Independence, Battle of Yorktown.
- **Important Figures:** George Washington, Thomas Jefferson, John Adams, and King George III.
- **Themes:** Causes of the revolution, major battles, the role of foreign allies, and the creation of the United States.

3. Formation of the U.S. Government (1783-1815):

- **Key Events:** Articles of Confederation, Constitutional Convention, Bill of Rights, War of 1812.
- **Important Figures:** James Madison, Alexander Hamilton, Thomas Jefferson, and James Monroe.
- **Themes:** Weaknesses of the Articles of Confederation, drafting and ratification of the Constitution, Federalist vs. Anti-Federalist debates, and early challenges to the new government.

4. Civil War and Reconstruction (1861-1877):

- **Key Events:** Secession of Southern states, key battles like Gettysburg, Emancipation Proclamation, Reconstruction Acts.
- **Important Figures:** Abraham Lincoln, Jefferson Davis, Ulysses S. Grant, Robert E. Lee.
- **Themes:** Causes of the Civil War, major military campaigns, effects of emancipation, and the challenges of rebuilding the South.

5. Industrial Revolution and the Gilded Age (1870-1900):

- **Key Events:** Rise of industrialization, labor strikes, immigration surge, urbanization.
- **Important Figures:** Andrew Carnegie, John D. Rockefeller, Samuel Gompers, and Jane Addams.
- **Themes:** Technological advancements, labor movements, economic disparity, and social reforms.

6. World Wars and the Interwar Period (1914-1945):

- **Key Events:** World War I, Great Depression, New Deal, World War II.
- **Important Figures:** Woodrow Wilson, Franklin D. Roosevelt, Winston Churchill, Adolf Hitler.
- **Themes:** Causes and effects of the World Wars, economic crisis and recovery, rise of totalitarian regimes, and global conflict.

7. Cold War Era (1947-1991):

- **Key Events:** Korean War, Cuban Missile Crisis, Vietnam War, fall of the Berlin Wall.
- **Important Figures:** Harry S. Truman, John F. Kennedy, Ronald Reagan, Mikhail Gorbachev.
- **Themes:** U.S.-Soviet relations, nuclear arms race, proxy wars, and the collapse of the Soviet Union.

8. Modern Era (1991-Present):

- **Key Events:** Gulf War, September 11 attacks, War on Terror, economic globalization.
- **Important Figures:** George H.W. Bush, Bill Clinton, George W. Bush, Barack Obama.
- **Themes:** Technological advancements, global terrorism, climate change, and political shifts.

CIVICS: UNDERSTANDING THE FOUNDATIONS OF DEMOCRACY

Civics education involves exploring the principles and structures that underpin democratic societies, providing individuals with the knowledge and skills to participate actively in civic life. This section will delve into key areas such as the origins of democracy, constitutional principles, citizenship, modern governance, and global affairs.

Origins of Democracy

To understand modern democratic systems, it is essential to explore their historical roots. The concept of democracy has evolved significantly since its inception in ancient civilizations. In ancient Greece, Athens developed one of the earliest forms of democracy, known as direct democracy, where citizens participated directly in decision-making. This model emphasized active citizen engagement and collective decision-making. Ancient Rome introduced a republican form of government with elected representatives, laying the groundwork for modern representative democracies. By examining these early models, learners gain insight into the foundational ideas of citizen participation and governance that influence contemporary democratic systems.

Constitutional Principles

Constitutions form the cornerstone of democratic governance, establishing the framework for government institutions and defining the rights and responsibilities of citizens. Constitutionalism emphasizes the rule of law, ensuring that all individuals and government entities are subject to the law. The principle of separation of powers divides government authority among the legislative, executive, and judicial branches to prevent the concentration of power. Checks and balances are mechanisms that allow each branch of government to monitor and limit the actions of the others, ensuring a balance of power and protecting individual liberties. By studying these principles, individuals understand the mechanisms that sustain democratic systems and safeguard freedoms.

Citizenship and Civic Responsibilities

At the heart of civics education is the concept of citizenship, which encompasses the rights and responsibilities of individuals in a democratic society. Active participation is a fundamental aspect of citizenship. Voting is a crucial right and responsibility, allowing citizens to influence government policies and leadership. Serving on a jury is another civic duty that ensures the justice system functions fairly. Beyond these formal responsibilities, citizenship also involves advocating for social justice, volunteering, and engaging in community activities. Exploring these aspects of citizenship empowers individuals to become informed and active participants in the democratic process, contributing to societal well-being.

Modern Governance: Institutions and Processes

Modern governance involves a complex network of institutions and processes that shape policy-making and the implementation of laws. The legislative branch, such as the U.S. Congress, is responsible for creating laws and consists of elected representatives who debate and vote on legislation. Understanding how a bill becomes a law, from proposal to enactment, highlights the legislative process and democratic decision-making. The executive branch, led by the president or prime minister, enforces laws, manages government operations, and conducts foreign affairs. Various executive agencies and departments carry out specific functions, such as national defense and public health. The judicial branch includes courts at various levels, from local courts to the supreme court. Courts interpret laws, ensure justice, and protect individual rights through judicial review and legal precedents. By studying these branches, learners gain a comprehensive understanding of the functioning and interdependence of government institutions.

Global Affairs: Interconnectedness and Challenges

In an interconnected world, understanding global affairs is crucial for addressing international relations and transnational issues. International relations involve interactions between states, non-state actors, and international organizations, aiming for peace, security, and cooperation. Diplomatic negotiations and conflict resolution are key components of maintaining global stability. Globalization has led to interconnected economies, societies, and cultures. Understanding the drivers and consequences of globalization helps address global economic challenges and fosters sustainable development. Transnational issues, such as climate change, pandemics, and terrorism, transcend national boundaries and require collective action and cooperation at the international level. Addressing these issues involves international efforts and mechanisms to ensure security, protect human rights, and promote global prosperity. Studying these aspects of global affairs equips individuals with the knowledge to navigate and address complex international challenges.

Navigating the Modern World

In conclusion, a comprehensive understanding of civics and global affairs enables individuals to become informed and engaged citizens. By exploring the principles of democracy, the functioning of modern governance, and the dynamics of global interactions, individuals are prepared to contribute positively to their communities and the world. This education fosters a commitment to justice, peace, and prosperity for future generations.

ECONOMICS AND FINANCIAL LITERACY

Economics and financial literacy stand as pivotal pillars within the realm of social studies, serving as indispensable components that empower individuals to comprehend economic systems, engage in informed financial decision-making, and participate effectively in the economy. This expansive section of the GED Study Guide Book embarks on a comprehensive journey through fundamental economic concepts, principles of financial literacy, and their practical applications in the real world.

Understanding Economic Systems

Economic systems, intricate frameworks governing resource allocation, production, and wealth distribution, unveil insights into the operation of economies and the repercussions of economic policies on individuals and societies. Diving into different economic systems unveils an understanding of the diverse approaches to economic organization and their impact on societal dynamics.

Types of Economic Systems

Capitalism, socialism, and mixed economies represent distinct paradigms in economic organization, each characterized by unique principles, incentives, and outcomes.

- **Capitalism**: Defined by private ownership, free market competition, and profit motive, capitalism facilitates economic transactions driven by market forces such as supply and demand. It emphasizes individual enterprise and fosters innovation and economic growth.
- **Socialism**: Socialism advocates for collective ownership or control of resources, aiming to achieve economic equality and social justice. Government intervention plays a significant role in redistributing wealth and ensuring social welfare.
- **Mixed Economy**: Blending elements of both capitalism and socialism, mixed economies combine market-driven allocation of resources with government intervention in specific sectors. This hybrid model seeks to balance individual freedom with social welfare.

Economic Indicators

Economic indicators serve as barometers of economic health, offering insights into the performance and trajectory of economies. From gross domestic product (GDP) to unemployment and inflation rates, these metrics provide a snapshot of economic conditions and inform policy decisions.

- **Gross Domestic Product (GDP)**: Serving as a yardstick for economic performance, GDP measures the total value of goods and services produced within a country's borders over a specified period. It offers insights into economic growth, productivity, and living standards.
- **Unemployment Rate**: Reflecting the proportion of the labor force actively seeking employment, the unemployment rate gauges the health of the labor market and indicates the availability of job opportunities.
- **Inflation Rate**: Tracking changes in the general price level of goods and services, the inflation rate informs individuals about the erosion of purchasing power and the stability of prices over time.

Principles of Financial Literacy

Financial literacy emerges as a cornerstone in equipping individuals with the knowledge and skills essential for managing personal finances, making sound financial decisions, and achieving financial goals. Cultivating financial literacy empowers individuals to navigate the intricacies of the modern economy and secure their financial future.

Budgeting and Financial Planning

Budgeting and financial planning lay the groundwork for financial stability and success, enabling individuals to allocate resources effectively and achieve their financial objectives.

- **Creating a Budget**: A budget serves as a roadmap for financial management, enabling individuals to track income and expenses, prioritize spending, and allocate funds towards savings and goals. It instills discipline and fosters responsible financial habits.
- **Financial Goals**: Establishing clear financial goals provides direction and motivation, guiding individuals in their pursuit of financial well-being. Whether aiming to build an emergency fund, purchase a home, or save for retirement, setting SMART (Specific, Measurable, Achievable, Relevant, Time-bound) goals facilitates progress and achievement.

Managing Credit and Debt

Prudent management of credit and debt is essential for maintaining financial health and avoiding pitfalls that can lead to financial distress.

- **Understanding Credit**: Credit literacy entails comprehending the dynamics of borrowing and lending, including concepts such as interest rates, credit scores, and credit terms. It enables individuals to make informed decisions regarding borrowing and repayment.

- **Debt Management**: Effectively managing debt involves assessing debt obligations, prioritizing repayment, and exploring strategies to reduce debt burden. By maintaining manageable levels of debt and making timely payments, individuals enhance financial stability and creditworthiness.

Savings and Investing

Savings and investing serve as cornerstones of wealth accumulation and financial security, offering avenues for building assets and achieving long-term financial goals.

- **Emergency Fund**: An emergency fund acts as a financial safety net, providing a buffer against unforeseen expenses or financial emergencies. Building an emergency fund cultivates resilience and minimizes reliance on credit during challenging times.
- **Investing Basics**: Investing entails deploying funds into assets with the expectation of generating returns over time. Understanding investment principles such as risk tolerance, diversification, and asset allocation empowers individuals to build wealth and achieve long-term financial goals.

Real-World Applications

The principles of economics and financial literacy extend beyond theoretical frameworks, manifesting in tangible applications that shape individual financial behavior, consumer choices, and economic policy. By translating economic concepts and financial skills into actionable strategies, individuals navigate economic landscapes with confidence and prudence.

Personal Finance

Personal finance encompasses a myriad of financial decisions and strategies that impact individual financial well-being and stability.

- **Financial Decision-Making**: Everyday financial decisions, from selecting banking products to choosing insurance policies, influence individual financial health and well-being. Applying financial literacy principles enables individuals to evaluate options, mitigate risks, and optimize outcomes.
- **Retirement Planning**: Planning for retirement involves setting aside funds and investing strategically to ensure financial security in later years. By leveraging retirement planning tools and vehicles, individuals pave the way for a comfortable and fulfilling retirement lifestyle.

Consumer Behavior

Consumer behavior is shaped by economic factors, social influences, and individual preferences, driving consumption patterns and market demand.

- **Informed Consumer Choices**: Consumer behavior, shaped by economic factors and psychological influences, drives consumption patterns and market demand. By exercising consumer rights and practicing discernment, individuals maximize value and uphold consumer welfare.
- **Financial Consumer Protection**: Regulatory frameworks and consumer protection laws safeguard individuals from predatory practices and fraudulent schemes in the financial marketplace. Familiarity with consumer rights and recourse mechanisms empowers individuals to advocate for fair treatment and redress grievances.

Economic Policy

Economic policy plays a pivotal role in shaping economic conditions, influencing financial markets, and driving economic growth and stability.

- **Government Intervention**: Government policies, spanning fiscal and monetary measures, exert a profound impact on economic conditions and financial outcomes. Understanding the implications of policy interventions enables individuals to anticipate economic trends and adapt financial strategies accordingly.
- **Global Economic Trends**: Globalization and interconnectedness amplify the influence of global economic trends on individual economies and financial markets. By monitoring global economic developments, individuals gain insights into emerging opportunities and risks in an increasingly interconnected world.

In conclusion, economics and financial literacy emerge as indispensable components of social studies education, equipping individuals with the knowledge, skills, and insights necessary to navigate economic landscapes, make informed financial decisions, and contribute to economic prosperity. By fostering economic literacy and financial empowerment, individuals lay the foundation for financial well-being and societal advancement in an ever-evolving global economy.

GEOGRAPHY AND THE WORLD

Geography serves as a foundational discipline within the realm of social studies, offering insights into the spatial distribution of phenomena, the interconnectedness of regions, and the diverse landscapes that shape human societies. This expansive section of the GED Study Guide Book delves into the multifaceted realm of geography, exploring the physical, cultural, and economic dimensions of the world and their implications for global understanding and citizenship.

Physical Geography

Physical geography delves into the natural features and processes that shape the Earth's surface, encompassing landforms, climates, ecosystems, and natural resources. Understanding the physical geography of the world provides context for human activities and environmental interactions.

1. Landforms and Topography

- Landforms: From mountains and valleys to plains and plateaus, landforms represent the diverse physical features that define Earth's surface. Understanding the formation and characteristics of landforms illuminates the dynamic forces shaping the planet.
- Topographic Features: Topography refers to the arrangement of landforms and elevation across a landscape. Topographic maps depict these features through contour lines, providing valuable information for navigation and land use planning.

2. Climatic Regions

- Climate Zones: Climate zones delineate distinct regions characterized by similar weather patterns and climatic conditions. From tropical rainforests to arid deserts and polar ice caps, climate zones influence ecosystems, agriculture, and human habitation.
- Factors Influencing Climate: Climate is influenced by various factors, including latitude, altitude, proximity to water bodies, and prevailing wind patterns. Understanding these factors elucidates the geographic distribution of climates and their impact on human societies.

3. Ecosystems and Biomes

- Ecosystem Diversity: Ecosystems comprise biotic (living) and abiotic (non-living) components interacting within a specific environment. From forests and grasslands to freshwater and marine ecosystems, biodiversity thrives in diverse habitats.

- Biomes: Biomes are large ecological regions characterized by distinctive plant and animal communities adapted to specific climatic conditions. Exploring biomes unveils the interconnectedness of ecosystems and the ecological services they provide.

Cultural Geography

Cultural geography is a multifaceted field of study that delves into the intricate spatial distribution of human cultures, traditions, languages, religions, and socio-economic practices worldwide. By examining these aspects, cultural geography provides valuable insights into the diversity and complexity of human societies across different regions and continents.

1. Cultural Diversity and Diffusion

Cultural diversity is a hallmark of human societies, reflecting the richness of traditions, beliefs, and practices that define various social groups. Ethnicity, as a central component of cultural diversity, encompasses shared cultural traits, language, ancestry, and traditions that bind individuals together into distinct communities. These ethnic groups contribute to the vibrant mosaic of cultures within societies, fostering a sense of identity and belonging among their members.

Furthermore, cultural diversity serves as a catalyst for cross-cultural understanding and cooperation, promoting empathy and respect for different ways of life. By celebrating cultural differences, societies can embrace the richness of human experience and foster inclusive environments that value diversity.

Cultural diffusion, another key aspect of cultural geography, refers to the spread of cultural traits, ideas, and practices from one society to another through various channels such as migration, trade, conquest, and communication. This process has been integral to human history, driving cultural exchange and adaptation across geographical boundaries.

Through cultural diffusion, societies have borrowed and assimilated elements from other cultures, leading to the enrichment and evolution of their own cultural landscapes. For example, the diffusion of food, music, art, and religious beliefs has contributed to the cultural hybridization observed in many parts of the world today.

Moreover, cultural diffusion has played a pivotal role in shaping the interconnectedness of global societies, facilitating interactions and exchanges that transcend geographical and cultural barriers. As cultures interact and influence one another, they contribute to the dynamic and ever-evolving nature of human civilization.

2. Language and Religion

Languages are not merely tools of communication but also repositories of culture, history, and identity. Across the globe, linguistic diversity reflects the richness and complexity of human societies. Language distribution maps offer a glimpse into this intricate subject, showcasing the myriad languages spoken across regions and continents. From the indigenous languages of the Americas to the diverse dialects of Asia and Africa, each language represents a unique heritage passed down through generations. Linguistic diversity fosters a sense of cultural pride and belonging among communities, highlighting the importance of preserving and promoting indigenous languages in an increasingly globalized world.

Religious Beliefs and Practices

Religion exerts a profound influence on human societies, shaping individual beliefs, communal values, and societal norms. Mapping religious adherence and sacred sites provides valuable insights into the spiritual landscape of the world and its cultural significance. From ancient temples and pilgrimage sites to modern places of worship, religious landmarks serve as focal points for communal gatherings, rituals, and celebrations. Moreover, religious beliefs and practices often intersect with social, political, and economic dimensions, influencing various aspects of daily life. Understanding the diversity of religious traditions and their geographical distribution, individuals can gain a deeper appreciation for the role of religion in shaping human culture and civilization.

Cultural Evolution and Adaptation

The study of linguistic diversity and religious practices also offers insights into the processes of cultural evolution and adaptation. Languages evolve over time in response to social, economic, and technological changes, resulting in the emergence of new dialects and linguistic variations. Similarly, religious beliefs and practices undergo transformations as societies interact and exchange ideas, leading to syncretism, reform movements, and religious revivalism. Scholars can unravel the complex interplay of cultural continuity and change, shedding light on the dynamic nature of human culture by tracing the historical trajectories of languages and religions.

Challenges and Opportunities

Despite the richness of linguistic and religious diversity, these aspects of culture also pose challenges in an increasingly interconnected world. Language barriers can hinder communication and cooperation among diverse communities, leading to misunderstandings and conflicts. Similarly, religious differences sometimes fuel sectarianism and intolerance, exacerbating social tensions and political instability. However, linguistic and religious diversity also presents opportunities for dialogue, exchange, and mutual understanding. Fostering intercultural communication and respect for diversity, societies can harness the power of cultural pluralism to promote peace, harmony, and cooperation on a global scale.

Urbanization and Settlement Patterns

- Urban-Rural Dynamics: Urbanization entails the growth and proliferation of cities, driving social, economic, and environmental transformations. Analyzing urban-rural dynamics elucidates settlement patterns, demographic trends, and urban sprawl.
- Megacities and Globalization: Megacities represent urban agglomerations with populations exceeding ten million inhabitants, serving as hubs of economic activity, innovation, and cultural exchange. Exploring megacities unveils the impacts of globalization and urbanization on human geography.

Economic Geography

Economic geography examines the spatial distribution of economic activities, resources, industries, and trade networks, elucidating the interplay between geography and economic development.

Natural Resource Distribution

Natural resources are essential components of global economic systems, with minerals, energy sources, water, and agricultural land being vital for sustaining human life and driving economic growth. However, these resources are not evenly distributed across the globe. Resource maps provide valuable insights into the spatial distribution of these resources, highlighting regions rich in natural wealth and their significance for economic development and environmental sustainability. Through understanding the geographic distribution of natural resources, policymakers and stakeholders can make informed decisions regarding resource management, conservation efforts, and sustainable development initiatives.

Resource extraction industries, including mining, logging, and fishing, play a significant role in meeting the growing demands of global economies. However, the extraction and exploitation of natural resources often come at a cost, impacting ecosystems, biodiversity, and local communities. Mining activities, for example, can lead to deforestation, soil erosion, and water pollution, posing significant environmental risks. Similarly, logging operations can degrade forest ecosystems, disrupt wildlife habitats, and contribute to climate change. Moreover, industrial fishing practices, such as overfishing and destructive fishing methods, threaten marine biodiversity and the livelihoods of coastal communities. Understanding these patterns of resource exploitation is crucial for addressing environmental degradation, mitigating negative impacts, and promoting sustainable resource management practices.

The extraction and exploitation of natural resources pose significant challenges to environmental conservation efforts worldwide. Unsustainable resource extraction practices can lead to habitat destruction, loss of biodiversity, and ecosystem degradation, threatening the long-term health and resilience of ecosystems. Moreover, the depletion of natural resources, such as freshwater aquifers and fossil fuel reserves, exacerbates environmental pressures and contributes to climate change. Addressing these challenges requires a holistic approach to environmental conservation that integrates principles of sustainability, biodiversity conservation, and ecosystem restoration. Through promoting responsible resource extraction practices and implementing effective conservation measures, societies can safeguard natural ecosystems, preserve biodiversity, and ensure the availability of vital resources for future generations.

The extraction and exploitation of natural resources also have significant social and economic impacts, particularly on local communities and indigenous populations. Resource extraction projects often lead to land displacement, loss of traditional livelihoods, and social conflicts over resource ownership and access rights. Moreover, the influx of migrant workers and the establishment of extractive industries can disrupt local cultures, social structures, and traditional ways of life. Additionally, the economic benefits derived from resource extraction activities are not always equitably distributed, exacerbating income inequality and social disparities within affected communities. Understanding these social and economic dynamics is essential for promoting social justice, upholding human rights, and fostering inclusive and sustainable development in resource-rich regions.

To address the environmental, social, and economic challenges associated with resource extraction and exploitation, policymakers and stakeholders must adopt comprehensive resource management strategies. These strategies should prioritize sustainable development, environmental conservation, and community engagement, while also promoting transparency, accountability, and equitable resource distribution. Implementing effective regulatory frameworks, environmental safeguards, and community consultation processes can help mitigate the negative impacts of resource extraction activities and ensure that natural resources are managed responsibly and sustainably. Furthermore, investing in alternative energy sources, green technologies, and renewable resource management practices can reduce reliance on finite resources and promote a transition towards a more sustainable and resilient global economy.

Given the transboundary nature of many natural resources, addressing the challenges associated with resource extraction and exploitation requires international cooperation and governance mechanisms. Collaborative efforts among nations, multilateral organizations, and civil society groups are essential for promoting sustainable resource management practices, preventing resource-related conflicts, and addressing global environmental challenges. Establishing frameworks for sharing scientific knowledge, best practices, and technology transfer can facilitate the adoption of sustainable resource management practices and promote cross-border cooperation in resource conservation and environmental protection initiatives. Working together, the international community can address the complex interplay of environmental, social, and economic factors shaping the sustainable management of natural resources and ensure the well-being of present and future generations.

Industrialization and Economic Development

- Industrial Zones: Industrialization clusters economic activities into specialized zones, such as manufacturing hubs, technology parks, and industrial corridors. Mapping industrial zones reveals spatial patterns of economic development and investment.
- Economic Disparities: Disparities in economic development, income levels, and standards of living persist across regions and countries. Analyzing economic indicators and development indices sheds light on the root causes of economic disparities and avenues for equitable growth.

Global Trade and Transportation Networks

Global trade and transportation networks form the arteries of the modern global economy, enabling the seamless exchange of goods, services, and capital across vast distances. This interconnected web of trade routes and transportation infrastructure plays a pivotal role in shaping economic globalization and fostering international cooperation.

Trade Routes:

At the heart of global trade are the various trade routes that crisscross the continents, facilitating the movement of goods and services between producers and consumers. Maritime routes, such as the ancient Silk Road and the modern-day Suez Canal, have long served as vital conduits for international trade, connecting markets across Asia, Europe, Africa, and the Americas. Similarly, air corridors and transcontinental railways have emerged as crucial arteries of global commerce, enabling swift and efficient transportation of goods and people across continents. These trade routes not only facilitate economic exchange but also foster cultural exchange and diplomatic relations between nations.

Transportation Infrastructure:

Central to the functioning of global trade networks is the robust transportation infrastructure that supports the movement of goods and people across borders. Roads, railways, ports, and airports form the backbone of this infrastructure, providing essential links between production centers, distribution hubs, and consumer markets. Well-developed transportation networks are essential for reducing transportation costs, minimizing transit times, and enhancing supply chain efficiency. Moreover, efficient transportation infrastructure is critical for attracting foreign investment, stimulating economic growth, and promoting regional development.

Assessing Transportation Networks:

Assessing and evaluating transportation networks is essential for informed decision-making in logistics planning and infrastructure development. By analyzing the efficiency, capacity, and connectivity of transportation routes, policymakers and businesses can identify bottlenecks, optimize supply chains, and enhance trade efficiency. Additionally, assessing transportation networks enables stakeholders to prioritize infrastructure investments, allocate resources effectively, and address emerging challenges such as congestion, pollution, and security risks. Furthermore, advancements in technology, such as real-time tracking systems and predictive analytics, provide valuable insights into transportation operations, allowing for proactive management and optimization of trade routes.

Enhancing Trade Efficiency and Connectivity:

Efforts to enhance trade efficiency and connectivity are essential for promoting sustainable economic development and prosperity. Investing in modernizing and expanding transportation infrastructure, such as building new roads, railways, and ports, can unlock new trade opportunities, stimulate economic growth, and alleviate poverty in developing regions. Additionally, fostering international cooperation and collaboration in trade facilitation initiatives, such as streamlining customs procedures and harmonizing regulations, can reduce trade barriers, promote cross-border trade, and enhance global competitiveness. Moreover, embracing digital technologies and innovation in logistics management, such as blockchain, IoT, and AI, can revolutionize supply chain operations, increase transparency, and reduce costs in global trade.

Global trade and transportation networks are indispensable drivers of economic globalization, facilitating the exchange of goods, services, and capital on a scale never before seen in human history. Through investing in robust transportation infrastructure, enhancing trade efficiency, and promoting international cooperation, nations can harness the power of global trade to foster economic growth, create jobs, and improve the quality of life for people around the world.

Geography serves as a multifaceted lens through which to explore the world's physical, cultural, and economic landscapes. Delving into the realms of physical geography, cultural geography, and economic geography, individuals gain a deeper understanding of the complexities and interconnectedness of the global environment. Embracing geographic literacy fosters informed citizenship, cross-cultural appreciation, and sustainable development in an increasingly interconnected world.

PART VII
TIPS AND TRICKS FOR THE GED EXAM

This part of this guidebook delves into a wealth of invaluable tips and tricks to empower you on your journey to success in the GED exam. As you navigate through this section, you'll discover a treasure trove of insights gathered from experienced educators, test-takers, and experts in the field, all aimed at equipping you with the tools and techniques needed to excel in each section of the GED exam.

From effective study methods to time management strategies, this section covers a wide array of topics tailored to address the unique challenges posed by the GED exam. You'll learn how to optimize your study schedule, identify your strengths and weaknesses, and develop targeted study plans to ensure comprehensive preparation across all subject areas. Additionally, we'll explore proven test-taking strategies designed to boost your confidence, minimize stress, and improve your overall performance on exam day. Some tips will be repeated from Part I to reinforce learning. Whether you're tackling the Language Arts (Reading and Writing), Mathematical Reasoning, Science, or Social Studies sections, these tips and tricks will provide you with the competitive edge needed to achieve your desired results.

With dedication, perseverance, and the insights gleaned from this section, you'll be well-equipped to overcome any obstacles and emerge victorious on exam day.

TEST-TAKING STRATEGIES

Test-taking, particularly in the context of high-stakes assessments like the GED, often evokes feelings of apprehension and uncertainty. The significance of such exams can weigh heavily on individuals, potentially impacting their performance. Yet, amidst this daunting landscape, there exists a realm of opportunity. Armed with the appropriate strategies and a well-structured preparation regimen, one can transform this intimidating challenge into a platform for success. It is within this transformative potential that we find solace and encouragement.

Understanding the Test Format

Before immersing ourselves in the realm of specific strategies, it is imperative to lay a solid foundation by acquainting ourselves with the intricacies of the GED exam format. The GED, a multifaceted assessment, comprises four distinct subject tests: Mathematical Reasoning, Reasoning Through Language Arts, Science, and Social Studies. Within each of these tests lies a myriad of question types, ranging from the conventional multiple-choice to the more interactive fill-in-the-blank, drag-and-drop, and extended response formats. Dissecting the structure of each test and acquainting oneself with the diverse array of questions is not merely a preliminary step; rather, it forms the bedrock of effective test preparation.

It is through this foundational comprehension that test-takers gain insight into the unique demands of the exam, enabling them to tailor their preparation efforts accordingly. Navigating the intricacies of the

GED exam format with precision and foresight, individuals pave the way for a more focused and targeted approach to study, setting the stage for optimal performance on test day.

Create a Study Plan

Crafting a study plan forms the basis of effective test preparation, serving as a beacon of guidance amidst the often tumultuous waters of exam readiness. Within the confines of a well-structured study plan lies the power to wield time and resources with precision, ensuring no stone is left unturned in the pursuit of academic excellence. Delineating a clear path forward, individuals can navigate the complex terrain of exam preparation with clarity and purpose, steadily inching closer to the pinnacle of success.

The genesis of a robust study plan lies in a deliberate process of self-assessment and introspection. Take stock of your academic strengths and weaknesses in each subject area, discerning areas ripe for further cultivation and those where your prowess shines brightest. Armed with this invaluable insight, proceed to map out your study sessions, breaking them down into manageable chunks, each imbued with a specific objective and goal. Through meticulous planning and goal setting, the amorphous task of exam preparation crystallizes into a tangible roadmap, guiding you towards your destination with unwavering resolve.

Throughout the process, remember that consistency is key. Stick to your study plan diligently, honoring your commitments with unwavering dedication and perseverance. Adhering steadfastly to the principles of your structured study plan, you cultivate a sense of discipline and resilience, laying the groundwork for success on test day. With each study session meticulously executed and each goal steadfastly pursued, you inch closer to the realization of your academic aspirations, fortified with the knowledge that you've left no stone unturned in your quest for excellence.

Read Carefully and Answer Strategically

When confronting multiple-choice questions, meticulous attention to detail is paramount. Begin by thoroughly parsing each question, extracting key phrases and nuances that may provide vital clues to the correct answer. Scrutinize each answer choice methodically, systematically eliminating any options that veer off course or deviate from the question's core premise. Employ the invaluable technique of process of elimination to whittle down the possibilities, leveraging your understanding of the question's context and structure to make an informed decision. In instances of uncertainty, trust in the process of elimination to guide your path, allowing for a calculated and educated guess that maximizes your chances of selecting the correct answer.

Conversely, when faced with fill-in-the-blank or extended response questions, meticulous attention to detail remains paramount. Begin by carefully parsing the instructions, ensuring a comprehensive understanding of the task at hand. Craft a response that is clear, concise, and directly addresses all components of the question, leaving no stone unturned in your quest for accuracy. Adhering steadfastly to the instructions and articulating your thoughts with precision, you cultivate a response that not only demonstrates your understanding of the material but also showcases your ability to communicate effectively under pressure.

Stay Calm and Focused

On test day, it's normal to feel nervous or anxious, but try to stay calm and focused throughout the exam. Take deep breaths, relax your body, and remind yourself that you've prepared thoroughly and are ready to tackle the test. If you start to feel overwhelmed, take a moment to pause, close your eyes, and center yourself before continuing. Remember to stay positive and confident in your abilities, and trust that your hard work will pay off in the end.

Review and Double-Check

Upon completion of the exam, allocate a few precious moments to meticulously review your answers, conducting a comprehensive audit to unearth any potential errors or oversights. Ensure that each question has been addressed with the utmost diligence and precision, leaving no stone unturned in your pursuit of accuracy. Verify that no question remains unanswered, leveraging your accumulated knowledge and critical thinking skills to tackle each query to the best of your ability. Should time permit, revisit any questions earmarked for review earlier in the exam, harnessing your newfound insights and clarity to scrutinize these queries with renewed focus and determination.

In the midst of this final review, cultivate a sense of trust in your instincts, refraining from unnecessary second-guessing unless unequivocal evidence of error emerges. Trust in the depth of your preparation and the clarity of your understanding, allowing confidence to permeate your every decision. With a sense of satisfaction and conviction, submit your exam, secure in the knowledge that you have poured your heart and soul into each response, leaving nothing to chance. Embrace the culmination of your efforts with pride and assurance, knowing that you have navigated the challenges of the GED exam with unwavering resolve and dedication.

MASTERING MULTIPLE-CHOICE QUESTIONS

With a significant portion of the exam comprising MCQ question types, candidates must hone their skills in deciphering, analyzing, and selecting the correct responses.

The Structure of Multiple-Choice Questions:

At the heart of mastering multiple-choice questions lies a deep understanding of their structure. Each multiple-choice question consists of a stem, which presents the problem or scenario, accompanied by several options, among which one is the correct answer. Familiarity with this structure allows candidates to deconstruct the question effectively, discerning the relevant information and clues embedded within the stem.

The stem of a multiple-choice question serves as the foundation upon which candidates base their responses. It may contain essential contextual information, critical details, or specific instructions guiding the selection of the correct answer. Thankfully, by analyzing the stem carefully, candidates can identify key elements, such as keywords, phrases, or numerical data, that inform their decision-making process.

In addition to the stem, the options provided in a multiple-choice question play a crucial role in the selection process. While one option represents the correct answer, known as the key, the remaining options, referred to as distractors, are designed to mislead or confuse candidates. Distinguishing between the key and distractors requires a keen eye for detail and critical thinking skills to evaluate each option's relevance and accuracy.

Reading Carefully

A cornerstone of mastering multiple-choice questions is the ability to read and comprehend the question stem accurately. Reading comprehension is not merely about skimming the text but rather engaging in a deliberate, analytical process to extract meaning and identify pertinent information.

Effective reading begins with a thorough examination of the question stem, paying close attention to the language, structure, and context provided. Candidates should read the stem multiple times, ensuring a comprehensive understanding of the problem or scenario presented. Moreover, they should identify any keywords, phrases, or qualifiers that offer insights into the intended answer or solution.

Furthermore, candidates must remain vigilant for subtle nuances or distinctions within the question stem that may influence their interpretation. Qualifiers such as "not," "except," or "only" can significantly alter the meaning of the question, requiring careful consideration and precise comprehension. Interestingly, reading the stem attentively and discerning its nuances, candidates can lay a solid foundation for effective decision-making when selecting their response.

Using Process of Elimination

In situations where candidates are uncertain about the correct answer, the process of elimination serves as a valuable tool for narrowing down the options and increasing the likelihood of selecting the right response. This strategic approach involves systematically eliminating implausible or irrelevant options, thereby reducing the pool of choices and improving the odds of identifying the correct answer.

The process of elimination begins by identifying and eliminating options that are obviously incorrect or incompatible with the information provided in the question stem. Candidates should focus on eliminating options that contain factual errors, logical fallacies, or inconsistencies, thereby streamlining the selection process.

Furthermore, candidates can refine their choices by comparing the remaining options against the criteria outlined in the question stem. By evaluating each option's alignment with the problem or scenario presented, candidates can identify subtle clues or patterns that indicate the correct answer. Even if uncertain, making an educated guess based on the process of elimination can enhance the likelihood of selecting the right option.

Avoiding Overthinking

While thorough analysis and critical thinking are essential when tackling multiple-choice questions, candidates must strike a balance between thoroughness and efficiency to avoid overthinking. Overanalyzing the question stem or fixating on minor details can lead to indecision or confusion, hampering the candidate's ability to select the correct answer effectively.

To avoid overthinking, candidates should adopt a structured approach to reading and analyzing the question stem, focusing on extracting relevant information and identifying key elements that inform the selection process. Maintaining a clear and concise thought process, candidates can streamline their decision-making and avoid becoming mired in unnecessary complexity.

Moreover, candidates should trust their instincts and rely on the knowledge and preparation acquired during their study process. While it's essential to consider all available options carefully, excessive second-guessing or self-doubt can undermine confidence and impede progress. By simply cultivating self-assurance and confidence in their abilities, candidates can approach multiple-choice questions with clarity and conviction, enhancing their overall performance on the GED exam.

Maximizing Efficiency and Productivity:

Effective time management is a critical aspect of success on the GED exam, particularly when navigating multiple-choice questions. With a finite amount of time allotted for each section of the exam, candidates must employ strategic techniques to optimize efficiency, productivity, and accuracy throughout the test-taking process.

Time management begins with a comprehensive understanding of the exam's structure, including the number of questions, time limits, and distribution of content across different sections. Candidates should familiarize themselves with the exam format and develop a pacing strategy that allows for sufficient time to answer each question while ensuring completion within the allotted timeframe.

Furthermore, candidates should prioritize questions based on their complexity, difficulty level, and relevance to the overall exam. Rather than becoming bogged down by challenging questions, candidates should adopt a flexible approach that enables them to allocate time proportionally to each question, maximizing their chances of completing the exam successfully.

Additionally, candidates should be prepared to make strategic decisions about when to move on from a particular question and when to invest additional time in finding the correct answer. Maintaining a balance between thoroughness and efficiency, candidates can optimize their time utilization and navigate the exam with confidence and composure.

Repetition and Review:

As with any skill, proficiency in mastering multiple-choice questions is cultivated through regular practice, repetition, and review. Candidates should dedicate time to engage in targeted practice sessions, utilizing sample questions, practice exams, and online resources to familiarize themselves with the question types, formats, and content encountered on the GED exam.

Practice sessions serve as invaluable opportunities for candidates to refine their test-taking skills, identify areas of strength and weakness, and gauge their readiness for the exam. Simulating exam-like conditions and constraints, candidates can acclimate to the pressures of the testing environment, thereby enhancing their confidence and performance on the day of the exam.

Moreover, candidates should adopt a systematic approach to reviewing their performance on practice questions and exams, analyzing their responses, and identifying areas for improvement. Identifying recurring patterns, trends, or errors in their responses, candidates can pinpoint specific areas of focus for further study and refinement.

Furthermore, candidates should leverage the feedback and insights gained from practice sessions to adjust their study approach, refine their test-taking strategies, and address any knowledge gaps or misconceptions. Incorporating feedback iteratively into their study regimen, candidates can continuously enhance their proficiency and readiness for the GED exam.

Ensuring Accuracy and Completeness:

Before submitting their exam, candidates should allocate time to review their answers systematically, ensuring accuracy, completeness, and coherence across all responses. The review process serves as a final opportunity to identify and correct any errors or omissions before the exam is finalized.

During the review phase, candidates should double-check each question and corresponding response, verifying the accuracy of their selections and confirming alignment with the information presented in the question stem. Additionally, candidates should pay particular attention to questions marked for review during the initial pass, ensuring that each question is addressed comprehensively.

Furthermore, candidates should assess the clarity, coherence, and organization of their responses, ensuring that they are logically structured and effectively convey the intended meaning. By reviewing each response critically, candidates can identify any ambiguities, inconsistencies, or errors that may require correction or clarification.

Moreover, candidates should be mindful of time constraints and allocate sufficient time for the review process without compromising the completion of the exam. Prioritizing questions that require further scrutiny and focusing on areas of uncertainty, candidates can maximize the effectiveness of their review and minimize the risk of overlooking critical errors.

With diligent study, practice, and preparation, candidates can conquer the challenges of the GED exam and achieve their academic goals, opening doors to a brighter future and broader opportunities for personal and professional growth.

STRATEGIES FOR OPEN-ENDED QUESTIONS

Open-ended questions, similar to MCQs, in the GED exam require more than just factual knowledge; they demand critical thinking, analysis, and effective communication skills. Whether you're tackling an essay prompt or a response requiring explanations, these strategies will help you navigate through these questions with confidence and success.

Break Down the Prompt

Before delving into your response, it's imperative to take a moment to thoroughly grasp the prompt. This involves dissecting the question into its fundamental components and discerning the task at hand. GED prompts often come with multiple facets or specific directives that necessitate meticulous attention. For instance, a prompt might task you with analyzing a historical event, evaluating its significance, and providing illustrative examples to bolster your analysis. Fully comprehending the prompt, you ensure that your response encompasses all requisite elements and remains focused. This comprehensive understanding enables you to tailor your answer to the prompt's demands, thereby presenting a well-rounded and coherent response.

Deconstructing the question is a pivotal step in effectively addressing open-ended inquiries. This process entails breaking down the prompt to unveil its underlying components and discerning the specific tasks or requirements outlined within. For instance, a prompt may entail analyzing a literary passage, identifying themes, and providing textual evidence to substantiate your analysis. Deconstructing the question, you gain clarity on its nuances and can formulate a targeted approach for constructing your response. This meticulous approach guarantees that you address all facets of the prompt comprehensively, minimizing the risk of overlooking crucial details. Investing time in deconstructing the question lays the groundwork for a focused and well-structured response, thereby enhancing your prospects of success on the exam.

Brainstorm Ideas

Once you've grasped the prompt, spend some time brainstorming ideas and organizing your thoughts. Consider various angles or perspectives from which you can approach the question. Jot down key points, relevant examples, and supporting arguments that you can incorporate into your response. This brainstorming phase allows you to explore different avenues of analysis and identify the most compelling arguments or examples to include in your answer.

Develop a Clear Thesis Statement

In essay-style questions, the formulation of a robust thesis statement assumes paramount importance. This statement functions as the cornerstone of your essay, encapsulating the primary argument or stance you aim to communicate in your response. It not only provides clarity and direction for your writing but also serves as a guiding beacon for both you as the author and your reader, navigating them through the intricacies of your argumentation. A well-crafted thesis statement possesses several key attributes that distinguish it as an effective tool for communication. Firstly, it should be specific, clearly delineating the focus and scope of your argument. Secondly, it ought to be debatable, inviting discussion and analysis rather than presenting a universally accepted truth. Lastly, a strong thesis statement is substantiated by evidence, drawing upon relevant facts, examples, or logical reasoning to support its claims. For instance, in response to a prompt exploring the impact of technology on modern society, a nuanced thesis statement might assert that while technology has undeniably revolutionized communication and productivity, its proliferation has also engendered concerns regarding social isolation and privacy infringement.

Crafting an effective thesis statement necessitates a meticulous consideration of the prompt and a judicious selection of key arguments and supporting evidence. It serves as a roadmap for your essay, providing a clear trajectory for your argumentation and ensuring coherence and cohesion in your writing. Furthermore, a well-articulated thesis statement not only guides your writing process but also facilitates comprehension and engagement for your reader. Clearly articulating your main argument and the rationale behind it, you invite your audience to actively engage with your ideas and perspectives. Moreover, a compelling thesis statement sets the tone for the rest of your essay, establishing the framework within which subsequent arguments and evidence will be presented and evaluated. Therefore, investing time and effort in crafting a strong thesis statement is a foundational step in the essay-writing process, laying the groundwork for a coherent, persuasive, and impactful response to the prompt.

Provide Relevant Examples

In constructing a compelling argument or explanation, incorporating relevant examples is paramount. These examples not only serve to bolster your points but also add credibility to your response and showcase your understanding of the topic at hand. It's crucial to select examples thoughtfully, considering their applicability to the prompt and their potential to strengthen your argument. For instance, when discussing the importance of environmental conservation, citing specific instances of successful conservation efforts or highlighting the consequences of environmental degradation in various regions can significantly enhance the persuasiveness of your argument.

Examples from personal experiences, historical events, literature, or current affairs can enrich your response in several ways:

- ➢ Illustration: Examples provide tangible instances that help illustrate abstract concepts or arguments.
- ➢ Credibility: Incorporating real-world examples lends credibility to your response, showing that your arguments are grounded in reality.
- ➢ Clarity: Examples make complex ideas easier to understand by providing concrete instances that readers can relate to.
- ➢ Persuasion: Well-chosen examples can persuade your audience by appealing to their emotions or logic.
- ➢ Relevance: Examples that directly relate to the topic at hand reinforce the coherence and relevance of your argument.

Selecting and effectively incorporating examples, you can strengthen your argument and make a compelling case for your perspective. These examples serve as evidence of your comprehension and mastery of the subject matter, enhancing the overall persuasiveness and impact of your response.

Use Effective Language and Structure

Paying meticulous attention to both language and structure is paramount to ensure the clarity and coherence of your response. It is essential to select precise vocabulary that accurately conveys your intended meaning, thereby minimizing ambiguity and enhancing the effectiveness of your communication. Furthermore, incorporating varied sentence structures adds richness and depth to your writing, captivating the reader's attention and maintaining engagement throughout the text. Transitional phrases serve as signposts, guiding the reader smoothly from one idea to the next and facilitating the flow of your argumentation. Additionally, organizing your response in a logical manner is key to presenting your ideas persuasively. Each paragraph should center around a single main point, supported by relevant evidence and analysis. This systematic approach not only enhances the readability of your essay but also reinforces the coherence of your argumentation, enabling your reader to follow your line of reasoning effortlessly.

A well-structured essay not only enhances readability but also fosters a deeper understanding of your arguments. Organizing your thoughts in a logical manner, you enable your reader to discern the connections between different ideas and concepts more easily. This, in turn, strengthens the overall impact of your response, as a coherent and cohesive structure provides a solid framework for presenting your ideas persuasively. Moreover, a well-structured essay demonstrates your mastery of the subject matter and your ability to communicate complex ideas effectively. It conveys professionalism and attention to detail, instilling confidence in your reader and lending credibility to your arguments. Therefore, investing time and effort in refining the language and structure of your response is essential for crafting an essay that not only informs but also persuades and inspires.

Support Your Arguments with Evidence

In analytical or argumentative responses, it's essential to support your claims with credible evidence and reasoning. Refer to relevant facts, statistics, expert opinions, or logical arguments to strengthen your position. Avoid making unsupported assertions or relying solely on personal opinions. Critical thinking and evidence-based reasoning are key to success in open-ended questions. When presenting evidence, be sure to contextualize it within your argument and explain its significance in relation to the prompt. This demonstrates your ability to think critically and evaluate information effectively.

Address Counterarguments

Anticipate potential counterarguments or opposing viewpoints and address them within your response. Acknowledging and refuting counterarguments demonstrates your ability to consider multiple perspectives and strengthens the overall persuasiveness of your argument. However, be concise in your rebuttals and focus primarily on reinforcing your own position. Addressing counterarguments, you demonstrate intellectual rigor and strengthen the credibility of your argument. This ensures that your response is well-rounded and addresses potential objections that may arise.

Proofread and Revise

Allocating time at the conclusion of your exam to review and revise your responses is a critical step in ensuring the quality and effectiveness of your answers. Take advantage of this opportunity to carefully examine each of your written responses, paying close attention to potential grammatical errors, awkward phrasing, or unclear passages that may undermine the clarity of your arguments. Identifying and rectifying these issues, you can significantly enhance the overall coherence and persuasiveness of your writing. Moreover, consider making necessary revisions to strengthen the organization and structure of your responses, ensuring that your ideas are communicated in a clear and concise manner.

Proofreading serves as a vital safeguard against overlooked mistakes or inconsistencies that may compromise the integrity of your work. Take the time to thoroughly review each response, focusing on refining your language and polishing your prose to convey your ideas with precision and eloquence. This final step is indispensable for presenting your best work and maximizing your chances of success on the exam.

Arguably, in proofreading your responses, you demonstrate a commitment to excellence and attention to detail, qualities that are highly valued in academic and professional contexts. Additionally, investing time and effort in refining your writing skills through regular practice and revision will pay dividends beyond the exam, equipping you with invaluable communication skills that will serve you well in future endeavors.

Time Allocation

Allocate your time wisely by considering the complexity and point value of each question. If you find yourself lingering too long on a single question, it's advisable to move on and revisit it later if time permits. Prioritize your questions based on their point value and difficulty, focusing your efforts on those you feel most confident about.

Managing your time effectively, you can ensure that you address all questions within the allotted timeframe and optimize your overall score on the exam. Efficient time allocation is key to navigating the exam successfully, allowing you to approach each question with clarity and focus while maximizing your chances of achieving your desired outcome.

Practice, Practice, Practice

Lastly, practice is key to mastering the art of responding to open-ended questions. Familiarize yourself with different question formats, practice writing coherent and persuasive essays, and seek feedback from instructors or peers. Honing your writing skills and familiarizing yourself with the exam format, you'll feel more confident and prepared on test day. Take advantage of practice exams and study materials available online or through test preparation programs. The more you practice, the more comfortable you'll become with the format and expectations of the exam, ultimately increasing your chances of success.

Generally, open-ended questions in the GED exam present an opportunity to showcase your critical thinking, analytical, and communication skills. Employing these strategies, you can approach these questions with confidence, articulate your ideas effectively, and maximize your chances of success. Remember to stay focused, stay calm, and trust in your abilities as you tackle each question with diligence and precision.

TIME MANAGEMENT DURING THE EXAM

With multiple sections to complete within a limited timeframe, effective time management strategies can make a significant difference in your overall performance. Here are some tips and tricks to help you maximize your time during the exam:

Know the Format and Content

Before the exam day, it's crucial to thoroughly understand the format and content of each section of the GED exam. This includes knowing the number of questions, types of questions, and allotted time for each section. Familiarizing yourself with these details, you can create a plan of attack for how to approach each section within the time constraints. For example, if you know that the Mathematical Reasoning section contains a mix of multiple-choice, drag-and-drop, and fill-in-the-blank questions, you can practice strategies for tackling each question type efficiently.

Practice Under Timed Conditions

One of the most critical skills for success on the GED exam is effective time management. As the exam covers multiple subjects and requires completing various tasks within a limited timeframe, mastering time management techniques is essential. Among the various methods to enhance time management skills, practicing under timed conditions stands out as particularly effective. Simulating the exam environment through full-length practice tests, candidates can develop a better understanding of their pacing, identify areas of weakness, and refine their study strategies accordingly.

Benefits of Practicing Under Timed Conditions:

> ➤ Simulates Exam Environment: Full-length practice tests replicate the conditions of the actual GED exam, providing candidates with a realistic experience of the time constraints they will face.
>
> ➤ Paces Your Progress: Monitoring the time spent on each question and section during practice tests allows candidates to gauge their pacing and adjust their approach accordingly. This helps prevent rushing through questions or getting stuck on challenging ones.

- ➢ Identifies Areas for Improvement: Consistently running out of time in specific sections signals areas where candidates may need to improve efficiency or strengthen their understanding of key concepts.
- ➢ Builds Stamina: Enduring through a full-length practice test helps candidates build the mental and physical stamina required to maintain focus and concentration throughout the entire exam duration.
- ➢ Refines Study Strategies: Insights gained from practicing under timed conditions can inform adjustments to study methods, such as allocating more time to challenging subjects or practicing specific question types to improve speed and accuracy.

Practicing under timed conditions is an invaluable tool for honing time management skills essential for success on the GED exam. Replicating the exam environment, pacing progress, identifying areas for improvement, building stamina, and refining study strategies, candidates can enhance their readiness and confidence for the actual test day. Incorporating regular practice under timed conditions into their study routine empowers candidates to approach the exam with poise, efficiency, and the best chance of achieving their desired outcomes.

Prioritize Questions

Not all questions on the GED exam are created equal. Some questions may be more straightforward and require less time to answer, while others may be more complex and time-consuming. To make the most efficient use of your time, prioritize the questions you feel most confident about and can answer quickly. This may involve scanning through the questions briefly before starting to answer them to identify which ones to tackle first. Prioritizing questions in this way, you can ensure that you're making progress through the exam at a steady pace, rather than getting bogged down on difficult questions and running out of time later.

Use Breaks Wisely

The GED exam incorporates short breaks between sections, offering candidates brief moments to recharge. To make the most of these breaks, it's vital to use them wisely. Rather than lingering too long, opt for quick, revitalizing activities like stretching or deep breathing. This approach ensures that you refresh your focus and mental energy without sacrificing valuable exam time.

Strategic use of breaks not only revitalizes the body but also enhances productivity. Avoiding excessive downtime, you can maintain peak concentration and efficiency throughout the exam. Returning to the test with renewed clarity, you're better equipped to tackle remaining sections with confidence, ultimately maximizing your chances of success on the GED exam.

Pace Yourself

Managing your time effectively during the GED exam is crucial for success in each section. It requires a careful balance of pacing to ensure that you can address all questions within the allotted timeframe. Vigilantly monitor the clock as you progress through each section, distributing your time evenly to cover all questions. The objective is to aim for consistent pacing, dedicating roughly equal time to each question to avoid spending too much time on any single one.

Should you encounter a particularly challenging question, it's vital to avoid getting bogged down. Instead of dwelling excessively, swiftly make an educated guess and proceed to the next question. Maintaining momentum is key, as every question carries the same weight in terms of points. Getting stuck on one question risks running out of time for the rest of the section, potentially compromising your overall performance. Adopting a strategic approach to pacing, you can navigate through the exam efficiently, ensuring that you allocate adequate time to address all sections thoroughly.

Strategic pacing not only facilitates comprehensive coverage of all exam sections but also mitigates feelings of rush or panic. Pacing yourself effectively, you can navigate the exam with confidence and composure, without feeling pressured by time constraints. This approach allows you to maintain focus and clarity, optimizing your chances of achieving your desired outcomes on the GED exam. Remember, effective time management is not just about completing the exam within the allotted time but also about doing so with precision and poise.

Skip and Come Back

Encountering a challenging question during the GED exam can be frustrating, but it's essential not to let it derail your momentum. If you find yourself struggling with a particular question, don't waste precious time trying to figure it out right away. Instead, skip the question and come back to it later if time allows. Many times, you'll find that returning to a question with fresh eyes after answering others will help you see it in a new light. Be sure to mark the question for review so that you can easily locate it when you come back. Strategically skipping and returning to challenging questions, you can ensure that you're making the most efficient use of your time and maximizing your chances of success on the exam.

Budget Time for Review

At the conclusion of each section of the GED exam, allocating time for review is a critical component of effective time management. This dedicated review period allows examinees to revisit their answers, ensuring accuracy and completeness before moving on. Double-checking responses, particularly on questions that were skipped or marked for review during the initial pass, is essential for identifying and correcting any errors or oversights. Prioritizing the review of uncertain or flagged questions, examinees can focus their attention where it is most needed, optimizing their chances of achieving the highest possible score.

Resisting the temptation to rush through the review process is imperative, as thoroughness is key to identifying potential mistakes. While the pressure of time constraints may be present, maintaining a deliberate and methodical approach during the review phase is crucial. Taking the time to carefully scrutinize each response increases the likelihood of catching any inaccuracies or omissions that may have occurred during the initial answering process. Exercising patience and attention to detail, examinees can mitigate the risk of overlooking critical information and improve the overall quality of their exam performance.

Incorporating a structured review strategy into the exam-taking process not only enhances the accuracy of responses but also serves as a safeguard against unnecessary errors. Budgeting time specifically for review at the end of each section, examinees can ensure that they are making the most efficient use of their allotted time. This strategic allocation of resources enables individuals to maximize their chances of earning the highest possible score on the GED exam, ultimately contributing to their overall success and achievement of academic goals.

Stay Calm and Focused

Maintaining a calm and focused mindset is paramount for effective time management throughout the GED exam. Anxiety and stress pose significant obstacles, impairing your ability to think clearly and act decisively under pressure. These negative emotions can disrupt your pacing, leading to rushed decisions and suboptimal performance. To counteract the detrimental effects of anxiety, it's essential to employ relaxation techniques. Deep breathing, visualization, and positive self-talk are effective methods for calming your nerves and centering your focus. Integrating these practices into your exam preparation routine, you can cultivate a sense of tranquility and confidence that will serve you well on test day.

It's important to acknowledge that feeling nervous before and during the exam is entirely normal. However, it's equally important to remind yourself that you have thoroughly prepared for this moment. Trust in your abilities and the work you've invested in your studies. Embracing a mindset of calmness and focus, you can approach each section of the exam with renewed confidence and clarity. This positive mindset not only enhances your ability to manage time effectively but also maximizes your chances of success. With a composed demeanor and unwavering concentration, you can navigate through the GED exam with poise, ensuring that you perform to the best of your abilities and achieve your desired outcomes.

Practice Time Management Strategies

Effective time management is a skill that can be honed through practice. Experiment with different time management strategies during your study sessions to find what works best for you. For example, try setting specific time limits for each section or question, breaking the exam into manageable chunks, or using mnemonic devices to help remember key information. The more you practice these strategies, the more comfortable and confident you'll become at managing your time effectively during the GED exam. Don't be afraid to adjust your approach as needed based on your performance and feedback from practice tests.

Seek Help if Needed

If you find yourself struggling with time management during your GED exam preparation, don't hesitate to seek help from a teacher, tutor, or study group. They can provide valuable insights, tips, and support to help you improve your time management skills and succeed on the exam. Consider reaching out to peers who have already taken the GED exam for advice on how they managed their time effectively. Additionally, many online resources offer tips and strategies specifically designed to help GED test-takers improve their time management skills. Seeking help when needed, you can gain valuable guidance and support to help you achieve your goals on the exam.

By implementing these time management tips and tricks, you can approach the GED exam with confidence, focus, and efficiency. Remember that effective time management is just as much about mental discipline as it is about pacing and prioritization. Staying organized, staying calm under pressure, and practicing strategic time management techniques, you can maximize your chances of success on the exam and earn your GED credential.

PART VIII

PRACTICE MAKES PERFECT, FULL GED EXAM SIMULATION

The GED test is a comprehensive examination designed to assess individuals' knowledge and skills across various subject areas. It comprises a diverse range of question types, including multiple-choice, fill-in-the-blank, drop-down, and extended response questions. Each question type serves to evaluate different aspects of a test-taker's understanding and proficiency in the respective subject matter. For example, multiple-choice questions assess comprehension and recall, while fill-in-the-blank and drop-down questions gauge problem-solving abilities and application of concepts. Extended response questions require test-takers to demonstrate critical thinking and communication skills by providing detailed written responses. This diverse array of question types ensures that the GED test effectively measures candidates' overall academic readiness and competence.

Structurally, the GED test encompasses various subject-specific exams, each with its own unique content and format. For instance, the Social Studies Test consists of 50 multiple-choice questions distributed across four content areas, covering topics such as history, geography, economics, and civics. Similarly, the Math Test comprises 45 to 49 questions divided into four main categories, including algebra, geometry, data analysis, and number operations. To pass the Math test, candidates typically need to answer between 30 and 32 questions correctly, demonstrating proficiency in fundamental mathematical concepts and problem-solving skills. Additionally, the Reasoning through Language Arts Test (RLA) assesses reading and writing abilities through approximately 46 questions, evaluating comprehension, analysis, and synthesis of written texts.

In addition to subject-specific exams, the GED Language test serves to evaluate candidates' language proficiency and communication skills. This test spans 150 minutes and consists of approximately 53 questions, covering three main categories: Grammar, Reading, and Writing. Within these categories, test-takers are assessed on their knowledge of grammar rules, comprehension of written passages, and ability to express ideas coherently through written communication. The GED Language test provides a comprehensive assessment of language arts skills, encompassing both foundational concepts and higher-order thinking abilities.

Successfully completing the GED Language test as a candidate, helps you demonstrate your proficiency in language arts and readiness for further academic pursuits or career advancement opportunities.

SIMULATING THE GED EXAM EXPERIENCE

Instructions:

- This simulated exam consists of four sections: Mathematical Reasoning, Reasoning Through Language Arts, Science, and Social Studies.
- Each section contains a variety of question types, including multiple-choice, drag and drop, fill-in-the-blank, select an area, and dropdown.

- The Language Arts section includes Reading Comprehension, Extended Response, and Language Conventions.
- Use the provided formula sheet for the Math section.
- A calculator may be used where indicated.
- Read each question carefully and choose the best answer.
- You may take breaks between sections, but time each section as you would during the actual exam.

Time Limits:

- **Mathematical Reasoning**: 115 minutes
- **Reasoning Through Language Arts**: 150 minutes (including a 45-minute essay)
- **Science**: 90 minutes
- **Social Studies**: 70 minutes

Reasoning through Language Arts (RLA) Practice Questions

Language Conventions

1. Which sentence correctly uses a semicolon?

   a. I like pizza; my friend prefers burgers.
   b. I like pizza my friend; prefers burgers.
   c. I like; pizza my friend prefers burgers.
   d. I like pizza my friend prefers; burgers.

2. Identify the direct object in the following sentence: "She baked cookies for the party."

3. Choose the correct possessive pronoun to complete the sentence: "The book belongs to ____."

   a. hers
   b. her
   c. she
   d. their

4. Which sentence uses correct parallel structure?

   a. He likes hiking, swimming, and to ride bicycles.
   b. He likes hiking, swimming, and riding bicycles.
   c. He likes hiking, swimming, and he rides bicycles.
   d. He likes to hike, swim, and riding bicycles.

5. Identify the coordinating conjunction in the following sentence: "I wanted to go to the movies, but it was too late."

6. Choose the correct pronoun to complete the sentence: "Tom and ___ went to the store."

   a. him
   b. his
   c. he
   d. them

7. Which sentence is grammatically correct?

   a. Their going to the concert tomorrow.
   b. They're going to the concert tomorrow.
   c. There going to the concert tomorrow.
   d. Thier going to the concert tomorrow.

8. Identify the antecedent of the pronoun in the following sentence: "Sara told Jane that she would be late."

9. Which sentence contains a dangling modifier?

   a. While jogging, the rain started to fall.
   b. The cake was eaten by the children sitting on the porch.
   c. After finishing the book, she watched the movie.
   d. Walking down the street, he noticed the trees were beautiful.

10. Correct the following sentence for parallel structure: "She likes cooking, jogging, and to read books."

11. Which sentence uses correct subject-verb agreement?

    a. The dog barks loudly in the morning.
    b. The dog bark loudly in the morning.
    c. The dogs barks loudly in the morning.
    d. The dog's bark loudly in the morning.

12. Identify the type of conjunction in the following sentence: "She will either go to the party or stay home."

13. Choose the correct form of the verb to complete the sentence: "I ____ to the store yesterday."

    a. go
    b. went
    c. gone

d. goes

14. Which sentence uses correct punctuation?

    a. Sarah likes apples oranges and bananas.
    b. Sarah likes apples, oranges, and bananas.
    c. Sarah likes apples oranges, and bananas.
    d. Sarah likes apples oranges and, bananas.

15. Identify the adjective in the following sentence: "The tall building stood out against the skyline."

16. Choose the correct pronoun to complete the sentence: "The winner of the contest was ___."

    a. him
    b. his
    c. he
    d. them

17. Correct the following sentence for subject-verb agreement: "The group of students is going on a field trip."

18. Identify the prepositional phrase in the following sentence: "The cat slept under the table."

Reading Comprehension

Read the passage below and answer the questions that follow:

Title: "The Power of Imagination"

In a world filled with constant noise and distraction, it's easy to overlook the quiet power of imagination. From childhood dreams to adult aspirations, our ability to envision possibilities shapes our lives in profound ways.

Consider the story of Amelia, a young girl growing up in a small town. Despite the limitations of her environment, she found solace in books and spent hours lost in imaginary worlds. These adventures fueled her curiosity and sparked a desire for exploration beyond the confines of her surroundings.

As Amelia grew older, her imagination became her greatest asset. In the face of adversity, she summoned the courage to pursue her dreams, embarking on a journey that took her to faraway lands and unexpected opportunities.

Yet, Amelia's story is not unique. Across cultures and generations, individuals have tapped into the boundless potential of their imagination to overcome obstacles and shape their destinies. Whether through art, literature, or scientific discovery, creativity knows no bounds.

In a society that often values logic over intuition, it's essential to recognize the transformative power of imagination. By embracing our imaginative faculties, we open ourselves to new perspectives and endless possibilities, ultimately enriching our lives and the world around us.

Reading Comprehension Questions:

19. What is the main idea of the passage?
20. How does the passage describe the role of imagination in Amelia's life?
21. What does the passage suggest about the connection between imagination and overcoming obstacles?
22. How does the author use Amelia's story to illustrate the broader significance of imagination?
23. What tone does the passage convey towards the subject of imagination?
24. What inference can be made about the importance of creativity in society based on the passage?
25. How does the passage characterize the relationship between imagination and exploration?
26. What is the significance of the phrase "boundless potential" in the passage?
27. Which literary device does the author primarily use to convey the theme of imagination?
28. What is the author's purpose in writing this passage?
29. How does the passage suggest that imagination can enrich both individual lives and society as a whole?
30. What effect does the use of Amelia's personal narrative have on the reader's understanding of the passage?
31. How does the passage challenge the notion that logic is superior to intuition?
32. Which word best describes the author's attitude towards the value of creativity?
33. How does the passage encourage readers to embrace their imaginative faculties?
34. What role does the setting play in shaping Amelia's relationship with imagination?
35. How does the passage suggest that imagination transcends cultural and generational boundaries?
36. What does the passage imply about the potential impact of nurturing imagination in individuals and communities?

Extended Response

Extended Response Prompt

Prompt: The debate over the implementation of universal basic income (UBI) has gained traction in recent years, with proponents arguing that it provides a safety net for all citizens and stimulates economic growth, while opponents claim that it discourages work and is financially unsustainable. Analyze the arguments presented in the following texts and write an essay in which you argue for or against the implementation of universal basic income. Use evidence from the provided texts to support your position.

Texts:

Text 1: "Universal Basic Income: A Safety Net for All"

Advocates of universal basic income (UBI) argue that it provides a crucial safety net for all citizens, regardless of employment status. By guaranteeing a basic level of income, UBI can reduce poverty and income inequality, offering financial security to those who are unemployed, underemployed, or working in low-paying jobs. Furthermore, UBI can stimulate economic growth by increasing consumer spending, as individuals have more disposable income to spend on goods and services. Additionally, UBI allows individuals the freedom to pursue education, training, or entrepreneurial ventures without the immediate pressure to secure employment.

Text 2: "The Economic Challenges of Universal Basic Income"

Critics of universal basic income (UBI) highlight several economic challenges associated with its implementation. One major concern is the financial sustainability of UBI, as providing a guaranteed income to all citizens would require substantial government funding, potentially leading to increased taxes or budget deficits. Moreover, opponents argue that UBI could discourage work, as individuals might be less motivated to seek employment if they receive an income without working. This, in turn, could reduce the overall productivity of the economy. There are also concerns about the potential for inflation, as increased consumer spending could drive up prices, eroding the purchasing power of the UBI.

Essay Structure and Organization:

37. What is the most effective way to organize the main points in a five-paragraph essay?
38. How does the use of transition words and phrases contribute to the coherence of an essay?
39. What strategies can be used to ensure a logical flow of ideas within a paragraph?
40. How does the introduction of an essay differ from the conclusion in terms of content and purpose?
41. What role does the thesis statement play in guiding the development of an essay?

Grammar and Mechanics:

42. Identify and correct the grammatical error in the following sentence: "She don't have any plans for the weekend."
43. Explain the difference between a dependent clause and an independent clause, and provide an example of each.
44. How does punctuation affect the clarity and meaning of a sentence?
45. Which verb tense should be used when writing about events that occurred in the past but are still relevant to the present?
46. Describe the rules for subject-verb agreement and provide an example of a sentence that demonstrates this concept.

Sentence Structure and Variety:

47. How can varying sentence structures enhance the readability of a piece of writing?
48. Identify the type of sentence (simple, compound, complex, or compound-complex) in the following example: "Although she studied diligently, she still struggled to pass the exam."
49. What is a dangling modifier, and how can it be corrected in a sentence?
50. Explain the concept of parallelism in writing and provide an example of a sentence that demonstrates parallel structure.
51. How can the use of active voice improve the clarity and impact of a sentence?

Word Choice and Vocabulary:

52. Discuss the importance of choosing precise and appropriate language when writing an essay.
53. What strategies can writers use to enhance the effectiveness of their descriptive language?
54. Explain the difference between denotation and connotation, and provide an example of a word with each type of meaning.

Unscored/Experimental Section

The following passage presents a character faced with a pivotal decision, exploring themes of choice, uncertainty, and personal growth. The questions assess comprehension, analysis, and interpretation of the text. Read and answer the questions that follow.

Title: "The Decision"

Sarah stood at the crossroads, the wind tugging at her hair as if urging her to choose. Before her lay two diverging paths, each shrouded in uncertainty and possibility. The sun dipped low on the horizon, casting long shadows that seemed to dance with the flickering light.

In one direction, the path stretched out into the unknown, winding through dense forests and rocky terrain. It whispered promises of adventure and discovery, of challenges to overcome and dreams to pursue. Sarah could feel her heart quicken at the thought of the journey that lay ahead, of the stories waiting to be written and the horizons waiting to be explored.

But in the other direction, the path was familiar, lined with familiar landmarks and memories etched into the earth. It beckoned with the comfort of the known, offering safety and security amidst the chaos of the world. Sarah could almost hear the voices of loved ones calling out to her, urging her to stay, to tread the well-worn path of tradition and convention.

As Sarah pondered her decision, she felt a sense of unease creeping over her. The weight of expectation bore down upon her shoulders, threatening to crush her spirit and imprison her in a life of conformity.

Yet, amidst the doubt and uncertainty, a flicker of determination ignited within her soul. She knew that whatever path she chose, it would be her own, forged with courage and conviction.

With a final glance back at the familiar path, Sarah took a deep breath and stepped forward, her feet carrying her towards the unknown. As she disappeared into the shadows, a sense of freedom washed over her, filling her with a renewed sense of purpose and possibility.

Reading Comprehension:

1. What is the main idea of the passage?
2. Which of the following best summarizes the author's argument?
3. What inference can be made about the character's motivations?
4. Which of the following statements is supported by evidence from the text?
5. How does the author use figurative language to convey meaning?
6. What is the tone of the passage?
7. What is the author's purpose in writing this passage?
8. How does the setting contribute to the overall mood of the passage?
9. Which of the following best describes the relationship between the two characters?
10. What is the central conflict in the passage?
11. What effect does the author's use of dialogue have on the reader?
12. How does the author develop the theme throughout the passage?
13. What is the significance of the passage's title?
14. Which of the following would be the most appropriate title for the passage?
15. What role does symbolism play in the passage?
16. How does the author use irony to create tension?
17. Which of the following statements best describes the structure of the passage?
18. What does the author imply about the future of the protagonist?

Writing Skills:

1. Identify the grammatical error in the following sentence: "She don't have any plans for the weekend."
2. What is the correct way to punctuate the following sentence? "The cat sat on the mat"
3. Rewrite the following sentence to eliminate the dangling modifier: "Walking to the park, the birds chirped loudly."
4. Which of the following sentences demonstrates correct subject-verb agreement?
5. What is the most effective way to organize the main points in a five-paragraph essay?
6. How can writers ensure a logical flow of ideas within a paragraph?
7. What strategies can writers use to enhance the effectiveness of their descriptive language?

8. Explain the concept of parallelism in writing and provide an example of a sentence that demonstrates parallel structure.
9. How does the introduction of an essay differ from the conclusion in terms of content and purpose?
10. What role does the thesis statement play in guiding the development of an essay?
11. How does the author use transitional phrases to improve the coherence of a piece of writing?
12. What effect does varying sentence structures have on the readability of a piece of writing?
13. Describe the rules for subject-verb agreement and provide an example of a sentence that demonstrates this concept.
14. How can writers effectively incorporate evidence from a text to support their arguments?
15. Discuss the importance of choosing precise and appropriate language when writing an essay.
16. How can writers use active voice to improve the clarity and impact of their writing?
17. Explain the difference between denotation and connotation, and provide an example of a word with each type of meaning.
18. What is the significance of including relevant details and examples in a piece of writing?
19. How can writers effectively structure paragraphs to ensure coherence and unity?
20. What strategies can writers use to revise and edit their writing for clarity and correctness?
21. How does the use of descriptive language contribute to the reader's understanding and enjoyment of a text?
22. Describe the process of brainstorming and outlining an essay before beginning the drafting process.
23. How can writers use transitions to signal shifts between different ideas or sections within an essay?
24. What techniques can writers use to engage the reader's interest and attention from the beginning of an essay?
25. How can writers effectively integrate quotations from sources into their own writing?
26. Explain the importance of revising and editing for grammar, punctuation, and spelling errors in a piece of writing.
27. Describe the characteristics of a well-developed and coherent paragraph.
28. What strategies can writers use to vary their sentence structures and lengths for stylistic effect?

Mathematical Reasoning Questions

Arithmetic

1. What is the product of 7.6 and 5.3?

2. Evaluate: 34×5843×85.

3. If $x - 7 = 15x - 7 = 15$, what is the value of x?

4. What is the least common multiple of 6 and 8?

5. What is the sum of 35 and 48?

   a. 73
   b. 83
   c. 63
   d. 58

6. If a package contains 12 cookies and you eat 3 of them, how many cookies are left?

   a. 15
   b. 8
   c. 9
   d. 5

7. If 1/3553 of a number is 24, what is the number?

8. If a recipe requires 2 cups of flour and you want to make 3 batches, how many cups of flour do you need in total?

   a. 5
   b. 6
   c. 8
   d. 12

9. What is the square root of 8181?

10. Express 75% as a decimal.

Algebra and Functions:

   11. Solve for x in the equation $2x + 5 = 17$.

   12. If $y = 3x + 4y = 3x + 4$, and $x = 2$, what is the value of y?

   13. Find the value of x in the equation $3(x - 4) = 15$.

   14. If $2y - 7 = 11$, what is the value of y?

   15. Solve for x in the equation $4x - 9 = 27$.

   16. If $2(3x - 1) = 10$, what is the value of x?

   17. Simplify the expression $2x + 3(x - 2)$.

   18. If $y = 2x + 5$ and $x = 3$, what is the value of y?

   19. Solve for x in the equation $5x + 8 = 33$.

   20. If $3(y + 2) = 21$, what is the value of y?

Geometry and Measurement:

21. What is the area of a rectangle with length 8 meters and width 5 meters?

22. Find the circumference of a circle with radius 6 inches. (Use π=3.14)

23. Calculate the volume of a rectangular prism with length 10 cm, width 4 cm, and height 3 cm.

24. Identify the type of triangle with side lengths 3, 4, and 5 units.

25. If the measure of angle A is 60 degrees and angle B is 120 degrees, what is the measure of angle C in a triangle?

26. Find the area of a triangle with base 6 inches and height 8 inches.

27. Calculate the perimeter of a square with side length 12 meters.

28. Determine the volume of a cylinder with radius 4 inches and height 10 inches. (Use π=3.14)

29. Identify the type of quadrilateral with angles measuring 90°, 90°, 90°, and 90°.

30. If the area of a circle is 64 π square units, what is the radius?

31. Calculate the area of a circle with diameter 10 inches. (π=3.14)

32. Determine the surface area of a rectangular prism with dimensions 6 cm, 8 cm, and 10 cm.

33. Find the volume of a cone with radius 5 meters and height 12 meters. (Use π=3.14)

Data Analysis, Statistics, and Probability:

1. The ages of a group of friends are: 20, 22, 24, 26, and 30. What is the mean age?

2. What is the median of the following set of numbers: 2, 5, 7, 9, 10?

3. If a fair six-sided die is rolled, what is the probability of rolling an odd number?

4. A bag contains 8 red marbles, 6 blue marbles, and 4 green marbles. What is the probability of drawing a blue marble?

5. The heights (in inches) of students in a class are: 62, 64, 66, 68, and 70. What is the range of heights?

6. The scores of a group of students on a test are: 80, 85, 90, 92, 95. What is the mode?

7. What is the mean of the following set of numbers: 4, 6, 8, 10, 12?

8. If a fair coin is flipped three times, what is the probability of getting exactly two heads?

9. A jar contains 12 red marbles and 8 blue marbles. If one marble is drawn at random, what is the probability of drawing a blue marble?

10. The ages (in years) of a group of people are: 25, 27, 30, 35, and 40. What is the median age?

11. A group of students took a math test, and their scores are: 85, 90, 92, 95, 98. What is the range of scores?

12. If a fair six-sided die is rolled twice, what is the probability of getting a 4 on both rolls?

13. In a survey of 50 people, 30 said they preferred chocolate ice cream. What is the percentage of people who prefer chocolate ice cream?

Science Practice Questions

Life Science

1. What is the basic unit of life?

    a. Cell
    b. Atom
    c. Molecule
    d. Tissue

2. Which organelle is responsible for energy production in a cell?

    a. Nucleus
    b. Golgi apparatus
    c. Mitochondria
    d. Endoplasmic reticulum

3. What is the process by which plants make their own food?

    a. Photosynthesis
    b. Respiration
    c. Fermentation
    d. Transpiration

4. Which of the following is NOT a type of blood cell?

    a. Red blood cell
    b. White blood cell
    c. Platelet
    d. Neuron

5. What is the function of the respiratory system?

    a. To circulate blood
    b. To produce hormones
    c. To exchange gases
    d. To digest food

6. What is the chemical makeup of DNA?

    a. Proteins
    b. Nucleic acids

c. Carbohydrates

d. Lipids

7. What is the primary function of the immune system?

   a. To regulate body temperature
   b. To fight off infections
   c. To digest food
   d. To produce hormones

8. Which of the following is a function of the skeletal system?

   a. To transport oxygen
   b. To produce energy
   c. To provide support and protection
   d. To regulate metabolism

9. What is the role of enzymes in biological reactions?

   a. To speed up chemical reactions
   b. To regulate body temperature
   c. To provide structural support
   d. To store genetic information

10. What is the function of the nervous system?

    a. To produce hormones
    b. To regulate body temperature
    c. To transmit signals between body parts
    d. To transport oxygen

Physical Sciences

11. What is the chemical symbol for water?

    a. H
    b. O
    c. H2O
    d. HO

12. Which of the following is a noble gas?

    a. Oxygen
    b. Hydrogen

c. Helium

d. Carbon

13. What is the pH of a neutral solution?

    a. 0

    b. 7

    c. 14

    d. 10

14. Which of the following elements is a metal?

    a. Carbon

    b. Sodium

    c. Fluorine

    d. Sulfur

15. What is the chemical formula for table salt?

    a. NaCl

    b. H2O

    c. CO2

    d. CaCl2

16. What is the difference between an element and a compound?

    a. Elements are made up of atoms of the same type, while compounds are made up of atoms of different types

    b. Elements are made up of molecules, while compounds are made up of ions

    c. Elements cannot be broken down into simpler substances, while compounds can

    d. Elements always exist in a gaseous state, while compounds can exist in different states

17. What is the chemical formula for glucose?

    a. C6H12O6

    b. H2O

    c. CO2

    d. NaCl

18. What is a chemical reaction?

    a. A change in the physical state of matter

    b. A process that converts one substance into another

    c. A process that releases energy in the form of light

d. A process that involves the movement of electrons

19. Which of the following is NOT a characteristic of acids?

    a. Sour taste
    b. Turns blue litmus paper red
    c. Releases hydrogen ions in water
    d. Feels slippery

20. What is the law of conservation of mass?

    a. Matter cannot be created or destroyed in a chemical reaction
    b. Energy cannot be created or destroyed, only transformed from one form to another
    c. The total pressure of a mixture of gases is equal to the sum of the partial pressures of the individual gases
    d. The volume of a gas is inversely proportional to its pressure at constant temperature

21. What is the SI unit of force?

    a. Watt
    b. Joule
    c. Newton
    d. Volt

22. Which of the following is a renewable source of energy?

    a. Coal
    b. Natural gas
    c. Solar power
    d. Petroleum

23. What is the acceleration due to gravity on Earth?

    a. 9.8 m/s^2
    b. 6.7 m/s^2
    c. 3.0 m/s^2
    d. 1.6 m/s^2

24. What is the law of conservation of energy?

    a. Energy cannot be created or destroyed, only transformed from one form to another
    b. Energy can be created from nothing
    c. Energy is always decreasing in the universe
    d. Energy is constant only in closed systems

25. What is the relationship between force, mass, and acceleration, as described by Newton's second law of motion?

    a. Force = mass × acceleration
    b. Mass = force × acceleration
    c. Acceleration = force / mass
    d. Acceleration = mass / force

26. What is the difference between speed and velocity?

    a. Speed is a scalar quantity, while velocity is a vector quantity
    b. Speed is measured in meters per second, while velocity is measured in kilometers per hour
    c. Speed is the rate of change of position, while velocity is the rate of change of distance
    d. Speed is always positive, while velocity can be negative

27. What is the principle of conservation of momentum?

    a. The total momentum of a closed system is constant if no external forces act on it
    b. Momentum is always conserved in collisions between objects
    c. Momentum is always conserved in explosions
    d. The momentum of an object is equal to its mass times its velocity

28. What is the definition of work in physics?

    a. The product of force and time
    b. The product of force and distance
    c. The product of mass and velocity
    d. The product of energy and time

29. What is the law of universal gravitation?

    a. Every object in the universe attracts every other object with a force that is directly proportional to the product of their masses and inversely proportional to the square of the distance between their centers
    b. The force of gravity depends on the size of an object
    c. The force of gravity is the same everywhere in the universe
    d. Gravity is the only force acting between objects in the universe

30. What is the definition of power in physics?

    a. The rate at which work is done
    b. The energy stored in an object
    c. The ability of an object to do work
    d. The resistance of an object to changes in motion

Earth and Space Science:

31. What is the outermost layer of the Earth called?

    a. Mantle
    b. Core
    c. Crust
    d. Lithosphere

32. Which of the following is NOT a type of rock?

    a. Igneous
    b. Sedimentary
    c. Metamorphic
    d. Organic

33. What is the process by which water vapor cools and forms droplets, leading to the formation of clouds?

    a. Evaporation
    b. Condensation
    c. Precipitation
    d. Transpiration

34. What is the main cause of tides on Earth?

    a. Gravitational pull of the Moon
    b. Gravitational pull of the Sun
    c. Earth's rotation
    d. Earth's magnetic field

35. What is the layer of the atmosphere where weather occurs?

    a. Troposphere
    b. Stratosphere
    c. Mesosphere
    d. Thermosphere

36. What is the difference between weather and climate?

    a. Weather refers to short-term atmospheric conditions, while climate refers to long-term patterns of weather in a specific area
    b. Weather refers to the temperature, while climate refers to precipitation
    c. Weather refers to atmospheric pressure, while climate refers to wind speed
    d. D) Weather refers to natural disasters, while climate refers to seasonal changes

37. What is the water cycle?

    a. The movement of water through the Earth's atmosphere, oceans, and land
    b. The process by which water changes from a liquid to a gas
    c. The process by which water is absorbed by plants and released into the atmosphere
    d. The process by which water freezes and melts

38. What is an earthquake?

    a. The shaking of the ground caused by the movement of tectonic plates
    b. The eruption of molten rock from a volcano
    c. The sudden release of energy in the Earth's crust
    d. The movement of air masses of different temperatures

39. What is erosion?

    a. The movement of sediment from one place to another by wind, water, or ice
    b. The process by which rocks are broken down into smaller pieces
    c. The process by which plants absorb water through their roots
    d. The release of carbon dioxide into the atmosphere by burning fossil fuels

40. What is the greenhouse effect?

    a. The trapping of heat in the Earth's atmosphere by greenhouse gases
    b. The process by which plants absorb carbon dioxide and release oxygen
    c. The depletion of the ozone layer by chlorofluorocarbons
    d. The process by which fossil fuels are formed

41. What is biodiversity?

    a. The variety of species in an ecosystem
    b. The total mass of living organisms in an ecosystem
    c. The amount of carbon dioxide in the atmosphere
    d. The rate of species extinction

42. What is the primary cause of air pollution in urban areas?

    a. Industrial emissions
    b. Agricultural practices
    c. Vehicle exhaust
    d. Deforestation

43. What is the greenhouse effect?

a. The trapping of heat in the Earth's atmosphere by greenhouse gases

b. The process by which plants absorb carbon dioxide and release oxygen

c. The depletion of the ozone layer by chlorofluorocarbons

d. The process by which fossil fuels are formed

44. What is the main cause of ocean acidification?

a. Deforestation

b. Carbon dioxide emissions

c. Oil spills

d. Overfishing

45. What is the difference between renewable and nonrenewable resources?

a. Renewable resources can be replenished over time, while nonrenewable resources cannot

b. Nonrenewable resources can be replenished over time, while renewable resources cannot

c. Renewable resources are always cheaper than nonrenewable resources

d. Nonrenewable resources are always cleaner than renewable resources

46. What is the primary cause of deforestation?

a. Urbanization

b. Agricultural expansion

c. Mining

d. Climate change

47. What is the ozone layer?

a. A layer of the atmosphere that absorbs ultraviolet radiation from the Sun

b. A layer of the atmosphere that traps heat from the Earth's surface

c. A layer of the atmosphere that contains high concentrations of oxygen

d. A layer of the atmosphere that contains high concentrations of carbon dioxide

48. What is sustainable development?

a. Development that meets the needs of the present without compromising the ability of future generations to meet their own needs

b. Development that maximizes economic growth at the expense of environmental protection

c. Development that focuses solely on environmental conservation

d. Development that benefits only a small portion of the population

49. What is the role of wetlands in the environment?

a. Wetlands act as natural water filters, removing pollutants and improving water quality
b. Wetlands provide habitat for a wide variety of plant and animal species
c. Wetlands help prevent flooding by absorbing excess water
d. All of the above

50. What is the main cause of global warming?

a. Deforestation
b. Ocean acidification
c. Greenhouse gas emissions
d. Ozone depletion

Social Studies Questions

History

1. Which event marked the beginning of World War I?

   A) The assassination of Archduke Franz Ferdinand
   B) The signing of the Treaty of Versailles
   C) The bombing of Pearl Harbor
   D) The Russian Revolution

2. The Emancipation Proclamation, issued by President Abraham Lincoln during the American Civil War, primarily aimed to:

   A) End slavery in the Confederate states
   B) Annex territory from Mexico
   C) Establish voting rights for African Americans
   D) Abolish the institution of slavery in all U.S. states

3. The Marshall Plan was a U.S. initiative designed to:

   A) Rebuild Europe after World War II
   B) Contain the spread of communism in Asia
   C) Provide aid to developing countries in Africa
   D) Promote economic growth in Latin America

4. The Magna Carta, signed in 1215 by King John of England, is significant because it:

   A) Established the principle of trial by jury

B) Limited the power of the monarch and introduced the concept of constitutional government

C) Granted religious freedom to Protestants in England

D) Ended the Hundred Years' War between England and France

5. The Battle of Gettysburg, a turning point in the American Civil War, took place in which year?

   A) 1861

   B) 1863

   C) 1865

   D) 1867

6. The Treaty of Versailles, signed in 1919, formally ended which conflict?

   A) World War I

   B) World War II

   C) The Korean War

   D) The Vietnam War

7. The Industrial Revolution began in which country?

   A) England

   B) France

   C) Germany

   D) United States

8. The Declaration of Independence was adopted in what year?

   A) 1776

   B) 1787

   C) 1812

   D) 1865

9. Who was the first President of the United States?

   A) George Washington

   B) Thomas Jefferson

   C) John Adams

   D) Benjamin Franklin

10. The Monroe Doctrine, declared in 1823, warned European powers against:

   A) Colonizing the Americas

B) Establishing alliances with Native American tribes

C) Expanding their territories into Asia

D) Interfering in the affairs of independent countries in the Western Hemisphere

Geography

1. Which of the following is the longest river in the world?

   A) Amazon River

   B) Nile River

   C) Mississippi River

   D) Yangtze River

2. The Great Barrier Reef is located off the coast of which country?

   A) Australia

   B) Brazil

   C) South Africa

   D) India

3. The Himalayas are located in which continent?

   A) Africa

   B) Asia

   C) South America.

   D) Europe

4. Which of the following is NOT one of the Great Lakes of North America?

   A) Lake Superior

   B) Lake Victoria

   C) Lake Michigan

   D) Lake Huron

5. The Equator passes through which of the following continents?

   A) North America

   B) South America

   C) Africa

   D) Asia

6. Which continent is known as the "Land Down Under"?

   A) Europe

B) Africa

C) Australia

D) South America

7. The city of Rome is located in which country?

A) Italy

B) Greece

C) Spain

D) France

8. Mount Everest, the highest mountain peak in the world, is located in which mountain range?

A) Andes

B) Rockies

C) Himalayas

D) Alps

9. The Sahara Desert is located on which continent?

A) Africa

B) Asia

C) South America

D) Australia

10. What is the capital city of Canada?

A) Ottawa

B) Toronto

C) Montreal

D) Vancouver

Civics and Government

1. How many branches of government are there in the United States?

A) One

B) Two

C) Three

D) Four

2. Who has the power to veto legislation passed by the U.S. Congress?

A) The President

B) The Vice President

C) The Speaker of the House

D) The Supreme Court Chief Justice

3. Which amendment to the U.S. Constitution abolished slavery?

A) 13th Amendment

B) 14th Amendment

C) 15th Amendment

D) 19th Amendment

4. How many total senators are there in the U.S. Congress?

A) 50

B) 100

C) 435

D) 538

5. The concept of "separation of powers" in the U.S. government refers to:

A) The division of powers between the federal and state governments

B) The division of powers among the executive, legislative, and judicial branches

C) The division of powers between the President and Congress

D) The division of powers between the federal government and Native American tribes

6. What is the role of the U.S. Congress?

A) To make laws

B) To enforce laws

C) To interpret laws

D) To represent the executive branch

7. What is the highest court in the United States?

A) Supreme Court

B) District Court

C) Appellate Court

D) Circuit Court

8. How many amendments are there in the U.S. Constitution?

A) 10

B) 20

C) 27

D) 50

9. What is the minimum age requirement to become President of the United States?

   A) 30 years old

   B) 35 years old

   C) 40 years old

   D) 45 years old

10. Which of the following powers does the President of the United States NOT possess?

   A) The power to pardon individuals convicted of federal crimes

   B) The power to declare war

   C) The power to veto legislation passed by Congress

   D) The power to appoint federal judges

11. **Who is considered the "Father of the Constitution"?**
   A) George Washington

   B) Thomas Jefferson

   C) James Madison

   D) Benjamin Franklin

12. **Which of the following is a right reserved only for U.S. citizens?**
   A) Freedom of speech

   B) Freedom of religion

   C) The right to vote in federal elections

   D) The right to petition the government

13. **What is the term length for a U.S. Supreme Court Justice?**
   A) 2 years

   B) 6 years

   C) 10 years

   D) Lifetime appointment

14. **The Bill of Rights is composed of the first how many amendments to the U.S. Constitution?**
   A) 5

B) 10

C) 15

D) 20

15. **Which branch of the U.S. government is responsible for interpreting the laws?**

A) Executive

B) Legislative

C) Judicial

D) Administrative

Economics

1. What is the primary function of the Federal Reserve System in the United States?

A) Regulating interstate commerce

B) Collecting federal taxes

C) Controlling the nation's money supply and interest rates

D) Providing social welfare programs

2. Gross Domestic Product (GDP) measures:

A) The total value of goods and services produced within a country's borders in a given period

B) The total value of goods and services imported and exported by a country in a given period

C) The total value of goods and services produced by a country's citizens, regardless of location, in a given period

D) The total value of goods and services produced by a country's government in a given period

3. Which of the following is an example of a regressive tax?

A) Property tax

B) Sales tax

C) Income tax

D) Capital gains tax

4. The economic system in which the means of production are privately owned and operated for profit is known as:

A) Socialism

B) Communism

C) Capitalism

D) Mercantilism

5. What is inflation?

   A) A decrease in the general level of prices for goods and services
   B) A sustained increase in the general level of prices for goods and services
   C) The total value of goods and services produced within a country's borders in a given period
   D) The total value of goods and services imported and exported by a country in a given period

6. What is the role of the World Trade Organization (WTO)?

   A) To promote free trade and resolve disputes between member countries
   B) To provide humanitarian aid to developing countries
   C) To regulate global financial markets
   D) To enforce international environmental treaties

7. What is the difference between a recession and a depression in economics?

   A) A recession is a short-term economic downturn, while a depression is a severe and prolonged downturn
   B) A recession is characterized by high inflation, while a depression is characterized by deflation
   C) A recession affects only one sector of the economy, while a depression affects the entire economy
   D) A recession is caused by government intervention, while a depression is caused by market forces

8. What is the purpose of trade barriers such as tariffs and quotas?

   A) To promote international cooperation and economic growth
   B) To protect domestic industries from foreign competition
   C) To encourage specialization and comparative advantage
   D) To reduce the budget deficit and national debt

9. Which of the following is an example of a public good?

   A) Private healthcare
   B) Public transportation
   C) Luxury goods
   D) Fast food

10. How does globalization affect the economy?

   A) It increases international trade and investment
   B) It decreases economic inequality between countries
   C) It reduces the need for government regulation of markets
   D) It leads to greater economic self-sufficiency and isolationism

COMMENT

PART IX
TEST ANSWERS AND EXPLANATIONS

REASONING THROUGH LANGUAGE ARTS (RLA)

Language Conventions

1. Which sentence correctly uses a semicolon?

   - Answer: a) I like pizza; my friend prefers burgers.
   - Explanation: A semicolon is used to link two independent clauses that are closely related in thought. The sentence "I like pizza; my friend prefers burgers" correctly uses a semicolon to join two related independent clauses.

2. Identify the direct object in the following sentence: "She baked cookies for the party."

   - Answer: cookies
   - Explanation: The direct object is the noun or pronoun that receives the action of the verb. In the sentence "She baked cookies for the party," the direct object is "cookies" because it is what she baked.

3. Choose the correct possessive pronoun to complete the sentence: "The book belongs to ____."

   - Answer: b) her
   - Explanation: "Her" is the correct possessive pronoun that shows ownership. The sentence "The book belongs to her" correctly indicates that the book belongs to her.

4. Which sentence uses correct parallel structure?

   - Answer: b) He likes hiking, swimming, and riding bicycles.
   - Explanation: Parallel structure requires that items in a list or series follow the same grammatical form. The sentence "He likes hiking, swimming, and riding bicycles" maintains parallelism by using gerunds (verbs ending in -ing).

5. Identify the coordinating conjunction in the following sentence: "I wanted to go to the movies, but it was too late."

   - Answer: but
   - Explanation: A coordinating conjunction connects words, phrases, or clauses of equal importance. In the sentence, "but" is the coordinating conjunction that connects two independent clauses.

6. Choose the correct pronoun to complete the sentence: "Tom and ___ went to the store."

   - Answer: c) he
   - Explanation: "He" is the correct subject pronoun to use in this sentence. The correct sentence is "Tom and he went to the store," where "he" is part of the subject.

7. Which sentence is grammatically correct?

   - Answer: b) They're going to the concert tomorrow.
   - Explanation: "They're" is the contraction for "they are," which correctly fits the sentence "They're going to the concert tomorrow." The other options use incorrect forms (there, their, thier).

8. Identify the antecedent of the pronoun in the following sentence: "Sara told Jane that she would be late."

   - Answer: Jane
   - Explanation: The antecedent is the noun that the pronoun refers to. In this sentence, "she" refers to "Jane," making Jane the antecedent.

9. Which sentence contains a dangling modifier?

   - Answer: a) While jogging, the rain started to fall.
   - Explanation: A dangling modifier is a word or phrase that modifies a word not clearly stated in the sentence. In "While jogging, the rain started to fall," it is unclear who was jogging. It should be revised to "While I was jogging, the rain started to fall."

10. Correct the following sentence for parallel structure: "She likes cooking, jogging, and to read books."

    - Answer: She likes cooking, jogging, and reading books.
    - Explanation: For parallel structure, all items in a list should be in the same grammatical form. The corrected sentence uses gerunds (verbs ending in -ing) for all activities.

11. Which sentence uses correct subject-verb agreement?

    - Answer: a) The dog barks loudly in the morning.
    - Explanation: Subject-verb agreement means the subject and verb must agree in number (singular or plural). "The dog barks loudly in the morning" is correct because "dog" is singular and "barks" is the correct singular verb form.

12. Identify the type of conjunction in the following sentence: "She will either go to the party or stay home."

    - Answer: correlative conjunction
    - Explanation: Correlative conjunctions are pairs of conjunctions that work together. In this sentence, "either...or" is the pair, making it a correlative conjunction.

13. Choose the correct form of the verb to complete the sentence: "I _____ to the store yesterday."

- Answer: f) went
- Explanation: The correct past tense form of "go" is "went." The sentence "I went to the store yesterday" is in the correct past tense.

14. Which sentence uses correct punctuation?

- Answer: b) Sarah likes apples, oranges, and bananas.
- Explanation: The correct use of commas in a list is to separate each item. The sentence "Sarah likes apples, oranges, and bananas" uses commas correctly.

15. Identify the adjective in the following sentence: "The tall building stood out against the skyline."

- Answer: tall
- Explanation: An adjective describes a noun. In the sentence, "tall" describes "building," making "tall" the adjective.

16. Choose the correct pronoun to complete the sentence: "The winner of the contest was __."

- Answer: c) he
- Explanation: The correct subject pronoun to use after a linking verb like "was" is "he." The correct sentence is "The winner of the contest was he."

17. Correct the following sentence for subject-verb agreement: "The group of students is going on a field trip."

- Answer: The group of students is going on a field trip.
- Explanation: "Group" is a collective noun and is treated as singular. Therefore, "is" is the correct verb form. The original sentence is already correct.

18. Identify the prepositional phrase in the following sentence: "The cat slept under the table."

- Answer: under the table
- Explanation: A prepositional phrase begins with a preposition and ends with a noun or pronoun. "Under the table" is the prepositional phrase in the sentence.

Reading Comprehension

19. The main idea of the passage is that imagination is a powerful force that shapes our lives, allowing us to overcome obstacles, pursue our dreams, and enrich both our individual experiences and society as a whole.

20. In Amelia's life, imagination serves as a source of solace, curiosity, and courage. Despite the limitations of her small town, she uses her imagination to explore imaginary worlds in books, which in turn fuels her desire for real-world exploration and helps her overcome adversity.

21. The passage suggests that imagination provides individuals with the ability to overcome obstacles by offering new perspectives and possibilities. Through imagination, people like Amelia are able to summon the courage to pursue their dreams and navigate challenges creatively.

22. The author uses Amelia's story to illustrate that imagination is not limited to individuals but is a universal human trait. By showcasing how Amelia's imagination helped her overcome challenges and pursue her dreams, the author highlights the broader significance of imagination in human life and achievement.

23. The passage conveys a positive and reverent tone towards the subject of imagination, emphasizing its transformative power and boundless potential to enrich lives and society.

24. Based on the passage, creativity is portrayed as essential to society, offering endless possibilities for exploration, discovery, and personal growth. It suggests that society benefits from embracing and nurturing creativity in individuals.

25. The passage characterizes the relationship between imagination and exploration as symbiotic. Imagination fuels the desire for exploration, while exploration in turn inspires new imaginative pursuits, leading to a cycle of discovery and growth.

26. The phrase "boundless potential" suggests that imagination has limitless possibilities and can transcend conventional boundaries, enabling individuals to achieve extraordinary feats and create new worlds of possibility.

27. The author primarily uses the literary device of anecdote or personal narrative (in this case, Amelia's story) to convey the theme of imagination. By presenting a specific example of how imagination has influenced an individual's life, the author makes the theme more relatable and impactful.

28. The author's purpose in writing this passage is to highlight the importance and power of imagination in human life and society, encouraging readers to embrace their imaginative faculties and recognize the transformative potential of creativity.

29. The passage suggests that imagination can enrich both individual lives and society as a whole by offering new perspectives, inspiring innovation, and fostering personal growth and exploration.

It encourages readers to tap into their imaginative faculties to enhance their own lives and contribute positively to the world around them.

30. The use of Amelia's personal narrative helps readers understand the passage by providing a concrete example of how imagination can shape an individual's life and overcome obstacles. It makes the abstract concept of imagination more tangible and relatable.

31. The passage challenges the notion that logic is superior to intuition by highlighting the transformative power of imagination. While society often values logic, the passage suggests that imagination, fueled by intuition and creativity, offers unique insights and solutions that logic alone cannot provide.

32. The word that best describes the author's attitude towards the value of creativity is "reverent" or "appreciative." The author holds creativity in high regard, emphasizing its transformative power and essential role in shaping both individual lives and society as a whole.

33. The passage encourages readers to embrace their imaginative faculties by highlighting the benefits of doing so, such as gaining new perspectives, overcoming obstacles, and enriching both personal experiences and society. Recognizing the transformative power of imagination, readers are encouraged to tap into their own creative potential.

34. The setting plays a significant role in shaping Amelia's relationship with imagination by providing both limitations and opportunities. Growing up in a small town with limited external stimuli, Amelia turns to books and her imagination to explore worlds beyond her physical surroundings. This setting fosters her imaginative pursuits and shapes her desire for exploration.

35. The passage suggests that imagination transcends cultural and generational boundaries by highlighting the universal human capacity for creativity and imagination. Amelia's story is presented as a testament to the fact that people from diverse backgrounds and time periods have tapped into the power of imagination to overcome obstacles and pursue their dreams.

36. The passage implies that nurturing imagination in individuals and communities can have a profound impact by fostering creativity, innovation, and personal growth. By encouraging imagination, societies can empower individuals to overcome challenges, pursue their dreams, and contribute positively to the world around them, ultimately leading to a more enriched and vibrant society.

Extended Response Essay

The implementation of universal basic income (UBI) is a contentious issue, with strong arguments presented by both proponents and opponents. After analyzing the arguments, I contend that the benefits of UBI outweigh the challenges, and it should be implemented as a means to provide financial security, reduce poverty, and stimulate economic growth.

Proponents of UBI, as presented in Text 1, argue that it provides a crucial safety net for all citizens, which is particularly important in an economy where employment can be unstable and wages often do not keep pace with the cost of living. By guaranteeing a basic level of income, UBI can significantly reduce poverty and income inequality. This is especially beneficial for those who are unemployed, underemployed, or working in low-paying jobs, as it offers them financial security and a better quality of life.

Furthermore, UBI can stimulate economic growth by increasing consumer spending. With more disposable income, individuals are more likely to spend money on goods and services, which boosts demand and supports businesses. This increased economic activity can lead to job creation and further economic benefits. Additionally, UBI provides individuals with the freedom to pursue education, training, or entrepreneurial ventures without the immediate pressure to secure employment, which can lead to a more skilled and innovative workforce.

On the other hand, opponents of UBI, as highlighted in Text 2, raise concerns about its financial sustainability. Providing a guaranteed income to all citizens would require substantial government funding, which could lead to increased taxes or budget deficits. While this is a valid concern, it is important to consider that the costs of UBI could be offset by the reduction in other social welfare programs and the economic growth generated by increased consumer spending. Additionally, innovative funding solutions, such as a wealth tax or carbon tax, could be explored to finance UBI without placing an undue burden on the general population.

Critics also argue that UBI could discourage work, as individuals might be less motivated to seek employment if they receive an income without working. However, evidence from pilot programs and studies suggests that UBI does not significantly reduce the incentive to work. In fact, it can encourage individuals to seek better employment opportunities, further their education, or start their own businesses, as they are not trapped in low-paying jobs just to make ends meet.

Concerns about inflation, raised in Text 2, are also worth considering. Increased consumer spending could drive up prices, potentially eroding the purchasing power of UBI. However, careful design and implementation of UBI can mitigate this risk. For instance, UBI could be adjusted periodically to keep pace with inflation, ensuring that it continues to provide meaningful financial support.

In conclusion, while there are challenges associated with the implementation of universal basic income, the potential benefits make it a worthwhile endeavor. UBI can provide financial security, reduce poverty, and stimulate economic growth, leading to a more equitable and prosperous society. By addressing concerns about funding, work incentives, and inflation, UBI can be designed in a way that maximizes its positive impact while minimizing potential drawbacks.

Essay Structure and Organization

37. The most effective way to organize the main points in a five-paragraph essay is to follow the traditional structure: introduction, three body paragraphs (each discussing a separate main point or argument), and a conclusion. Each body paragraph should start with a topic sentence, followed by supporting details or evidence, and end with a concluding sentence that transitions to the next paragraph.

38. Transition words and phrases contribute to the coherence of an essay by signaling the relationship between ideas and helping readers understand the flow of the text. They provide smooth transitions between sentences and paragraphs, guiding the reader through the argument or narrative. Examples include "however," "in addition," "furthermore," "therefore," and "conversely."

39. Strategies to ensure a logical flow of ideas within a paragraph include using topic sentences to introduce the main point, providing supporting evidence or examples, using transitions to connect ideas, and maintaining a clear and consistent focus on the topic. Additionally, arranging ideas in a logical order and using parallel structure can help improve coherence within a paragraph.

40. The introduction of an essay typically presents the topic or thesis statement, provides background information or context, and outlines the main points to be discussed. Its purpose is to engage the reader and set the direction for the essay. In contrast, the conclusion summarizes the main points, restates the thesis, and often provides a final thought or recommendation. Its purpose is to leave a lasting impression on the reader and reinforce the significance of the essay's argument or findings.

41. The thesis statement plays a crucial role in guiding the development of an essay by presenting the main argument or claim and outlining the scope of the discussion. It provides a roadmap for the reader, indicating what to expect in the essay and guiding the writer in organizing and developing the supporting points.

Grammar and Mechanics:

42. The grammatical error in the sentence "She don't have any plans for the weekend" is the incorrect verb form. "Don't" is the contraction for "do not," which is used with the pronouns "I," "you," "we," and "they." The correct form should be "doesn't," which is the contraction for "does not" and is used with the pronoun "she." So, the corrected sentence is: "She doesn't have any plans for the weekend."

43. A dependent clause is a group of words that contains a subject and a verb but cannot stand alone as a complete sentence because it does not express a complete thought. An independent clause, on the other hand, is a group of words that contains a subject and a verb and expresses a complete thought, capable of standing alone as a sentence. Example:

- Complete Sentence: "Although she studied diligently, she still struggled to pass the exam."
- Dependent clause: "Although she studied diligently" (cannot stand alone)
- Independent clause: "She still struggled to pass the exam." (can stand alone)

44. Punctuation affects the clarity and meaning of a sentence by indicating the structure and relationships between words, phrases, and clauses. For example, the placement of commas can change the meaning of a sentence, and the use of periods and semicolons can signal the end of a thought or the separation of independent clauses.

45. When writing about events that occurred in the past but are still relevant to the present, the present perfect tense is typically used. This tense indicates that the action started in the past and continues into the present or has a connection to the present. Example: "I have visited Paris three times."

46. Subject-verb agreement means that a singular subject requires a singular verb, and a plural subject requires a plural verb. For example, "The dog barks" (singular subject "dog" matches singular verb "barks") and "The dogs bark" (plural subject "dogs" matches plural verb "bark").

Sentence Structure and Variety:

47. Varying sentence structures enhances the readability of a piece of writing by adding rhythm, flow, and interest. It prevents monotony and engages the reader by providing a mix of short and long sentences, simple and complex constructions, and varied sentence beginnings.

48. The example "Although she studied diligently, she still struggled to pass the exam" is a complex sentence. It contains one independent clause ("she still struggled to pass the exam") and one dependent clause ("Although she studied diligently").

49. A dangling modifier is a word or phrase that does not clearly and logically modify the intended word or phrase in a sentence. To correct a dangling modifier, it's necessary to rephrase the sentence to ensure that the modifier is correctly attached to the word it is meant to modify. Example of a dangling modifier: "Running down the street, my keys were found." (The modifier "Running down the street" does not logically modify "my keys." It should be corrected to: "While I was running down the street, I found my keys.")

50. Parallelism in writing refers to using the same grammatical structure or pattern for similar elements within a sentence or paragraph. This creates balance and clarity, making it easier for the reader to understand the relationship between ideas. Example of parallel structure: "She enjoys hiking, swimming, and biking." (Each item in the list follows the same grammatical pattern: verb + gerund.)

51. Active voice improves the clarity and impact of a sentence by making the subject of the sentence the doer of the action, which typically results in clearer, more direct, and more engaging writing. It emphasizes agency and responsibility, leading to stronger, more dynamic prose.

Word Choice and Vocabulary:

52. Choosing precise and appropriate language is important in essay writing because it helps convey the intended message clearly and effectively. Precise language eliminates ambiguity and ensures that the reader understands the writer's meaning, while appropriate language considers the audience, purpose, and context of the writing.

53. Writers can enhance the effectiveness of their descriptive language by appealing to the senses, using vivid imagery, selecting specific details, and employing figurative language such as similes, metaphors, and personification. Descriptive language should create a vivid and engaging picture in the reader's mind, evoking emotions and immersing them in the narrative or argument.

54. Denotation refers to the literal or dictionary definition of a word, while connotation refers to the associated feelings, emotions, or ideas that a word carries beyond its literal meaning. For example, the word "home" denotes a physical place where one lives, but it may connote feelings of warmth, security, and belonging.

Unscored/Experimental Section

Reading Comprehension Questions

1. The main idea of the passage is that the character, Sarah, is faced with a pivotal decision between the familiar path of tradition and convention and the unknown path of adventure and discovery. It explores themes of choice, uncertainty, and personal growth.

2. The best summary of the author's argument is that Sarah is torn between the safety of the familiar path and the excitement of the unknown journey. Despite feeling the weight of expectation and the comfort of tradition, she ultimately chooses to follow her own path with courage and conviction.

3. An inference about the character's motivations is that Sarah is driven by a desire for personal freedom, growth, and self-discovery. She feels the pressure to conform to societal expectations but ultimately chooses to pursue her own path, fueled by determination and a sense of purpose.

4. A statement supported by evidence from the text is: "Sarah pondered her decision, feeling a sense of unease creeping over her." This is supported by the passage's description of Sarah's internal struggle and uncertainty as she weighs her options.

5. The author uses figurative language, such as metaphor and personification, to convey meaning. For example, the wind "tugging at her hair as if urging her to choose" personifies the wind, giving it human-like qualities to emphasize its influence on Sarah's decision-making process.

6. The tone of the passage is contemplative and introspective, conveying Sarah's internal conflict and the weight of her decision. It is also hopeful and empowering, as Sarah ultimately chooses to follow her own path despite the uncertainty.

7. The author's purpose in writing this passage is to explore the theme of choice and personal growth, as well as the tension between tradition and adventure. It encourages readers to reflect on their own choices and the importance of following one's own path with courage and conviction.

8. The setting contributes to the overall mood of the passage by creating a sense of atmosphere and ambiance. The description of the crossroads, with the wind tugging at Sarah's hair and the sun dipping low on the horizon, adds to the sense of uncertainty and possibility, enhancing the mood of contemplation and introspection.

9. The passage does not explicitly mention two characters. Sarah is the only character mentioned, and her internal conflict drives the narrative.

10. The central conflict in the passage is Sarah's internal struggle between choosing the familiar path of tradition and convention or the unknown path of adventure and discovery. This conflict represents the broader theme of choice and personal growth.

11. The author's use of dialogue is minimal in this passage. There are no direct conversations between characters. Instead, the passage focuses on Sarah's internal thoughts and reflections, which allow the reader to empathize with her struggle and decision-making process.

12. The author develops the theme throughout the passage by portraying Sarah's internal conflict and the factors influencing her decision. Through vivid imagery and introspective narration, the author highlights Sarah's struggle to balance societal expectations with her own desires for personal freedom and growth.

13. The significance of the passage's title, "The Decision," is that it reflects the central theme of the passage: Sarah's pivotal decision between the familiar and the unknown, tradition and adventure.

14. The most appropriate title for the passage would be "Sarah's Choice: Tradition vs. Adventure" or "The Crossroads of Sarah's Life."

15. Symbolism plays a role in the passage through the crossroads, which symbolize the choice and uncertainty that Sarah faces. The familiar path represents tradition and convention, while the unknown path represents adventure and self-discovery.

16. The author uses irony to create tension by juxtaposing Sarah's feelings of unease and uncertainty with her eventual sense of freedom and purpose. Despite the initial discomfort of her decision, Sarah ultimately feels liberated by following her own path.

17. The structure of the passage is primarily descriptive and introspective, focusing on Sarah's internal conflict and decision-making process. It follows a chronological sequence of events, starting with Sarah standing at the crossroads and ending with her choice to follow the unknown path.

18. The author implies that the protagonist, Sarah, has chosen a path of personal growth and self-discovery. By following the unknown path with courage and conviction, Sarah embarks on a journey that will lead to new experiences, challenges, and opportunities for growth.

Writing Skills

1. The grammatical error in the sentence "She don't have any plans for the weekend" is the incorrect verb form. "Don't" is the contraction for "do not," which is used with the pronouns "I," "you," "we," and "they." The correct form should be "doesn't," which is the contraction for "does not" and is used with the pronoun "she." So, the corrected sentence is: "She doesn't have any plans for the weekend."

2. The correct way to punctuate the sentence "The cat sat on the mat" would be to add a period at the end, as it is a complete sentence: "The cat sat on the mat."

3. To eliminate the dangling modifier in the sentence "Walking to the park, the birds chirped loudly," you can rewrite it as: "As she walked to the park, she heard the birds chirping loudly."

4. The sentence that demonstrates correct subject-verb agreement is: "The students are studying for their exams." (The plural subject "students" matches the plural verb "are studying.")

5. The most effective way to organize the main points in a five-paragraph essay is to follow the traditional structure: introduction, three body paragraphs (each discussing a separate main point or argument), and a conclusion. Each body paragraph should start with a topic sentence, followed by supporting details or evidence, and end with a concluding sentence that transitions to the next paragraph.

6. Writers can ensure a logical flow of ideas within a paragraph by using topic sentences to introduce the main point, providing supporting evidence or examples, using transitions to connect ideas, and maintaining a clear and consistent focus on the topic. Additionally, arranging ideas in a logical order and using parallel structure can help improve coherence within a paragraph.

7. Writers can enhance the effectiveness of their descriptive language by appealing to the senses, using vivid imagery, selecting specific details, and employing figurative language such as similes, metaphors, and personification. Descriptive language should create a vivid and engaging picture in the reader's mind, evoking emotions and immersing them in the narrative or argument.

8. Parallelism in writing refers to using the same grammatical structure or pattern for similar elements within a sentence or paragraph. This creates balance and clarity, making it easier for the reader to understand the relationship between ideas. Example of parallel structure: "She enjoys hiking, swimming, and biking." (Each item in the list follows the same grammatical pattern: verb + gerund.)

9. The introduction of an essay typically presents the topic or thesis statement, provides background information or context, and outlines the main points to be discussed. Its purpose is to engage the reader and set the direction for the essay. In contrast, the conclusion summarizes the main points, restates the thesis, and often provides a final thought or recommendation. Its purpose is to leave a lasting impression on the reader and reinforce the significance of the essay's argument or findings.

10. The thesis statement plays a crucial role in guiding the development of an essay by presenting the main argument or claim and outlining the scope of the discussion. It provides a roadmap for the reader, indicating what to expect in the essay and guiding the writer in organizing and developing the supporting points.

11. Authors use transitional phrases to improve the coherence of a piece of writing by signaling the relationship between ideas and helping readers understand the flow of the text. They provide smooth transitions between sentences and paragraphs, guiding the reader through the argument or narrative. Examples include "however," "in addition," "furthermore," "therefore," and "conversely."

12. Varying sentence structures has a positive effect on the readability of a piece of writing by adding rhythm, flow, and interest. It prevents monotony and engages the reader by providing a mix of short and long sentences, simple and complex constructions, and varied sentence beginnings.

13. Subject-verb agreement means that a singular subject requires a singular verb, and a plural subject requires a plural verb. For example, "The dog barks" (singular subject "dog" matches singular verb "barks") and "The dogs bark" (plural subject "dogs" matches plural verb "bark").

14. Writers can effectively incorporate evidence from a text to support their arguments by quoting directly from the text, summarizing key points, and paraphrasing information in their own words. It's important to provide context for the evidence, analyze its relevance to the argument, and cite the source properly to maintain credibility.

15. Choosing precise and appropriate language is important in essay writing because it helps convey the intended message clearly and effectively. Precise language eliminates ambiguity and ensures that the reader understands the writer's meaning, while appropriate language considers the audience, purpose, and context of the writing.

16. Writers can use active voice to improve the clarity and impact of their writing by making the subject of the sentence the doer of the action. Active voice sentences are generally clearer, more direct, and more engaging than passive voice sentences. For example, "The cat chased the mouse" (active voice) versus "The mouse was chased by the cat" (passive voice).

17. Denotation refers to the literal or dictionary definition of a word, while connotation refers to the associated feelings, emotions, or ideas that a word carries beyond its literal meaning. For example, the word "home" denotes a physical place where one lives, but it may connote feelings of warmth, security, and belonging.

18. The significance of including relevant details and examples in a piece of writing is that it strengthens the argument, provides evidence to support claims, and engages the reader by making the writing more vivid and persuasive. Relevant details and examples help clarify abstract concepts, illustrate complex ideas, and make the writing more relatable to the reader's experiences.

19. Writers can effectively structure paragraphs to ensure coherence and unity by following a clear topic sentence, providing supporting details or evidence, using transitions to connect ideas, and maintaining a consistent focus on the main topic or argument. Each paragraph should present a unified idea or theme, and the order of ideas should flow logically from one to the next.

20. Strategies writers can use to revise and edit their writing for clarity and correctness include reading the text aloud, checking for grammatical errors and punctuation mistakes, reviewing sentence structure and word choice, seeking feedback from peers or instructors, and using editing tools such as spell checkers and grammar checkers.

21. Descriptive language contributes to the reader's understanding and enjoyment of a text by creating vivid imagery, evoking emotions, and immersing the reader in the narrative or argument. Descriptive language helps paint a picture in the reader's mind, making the writing more engaging, memorable, and impactful.

22. Brainstorming involves generating ideas and gathering information on a topic before beginning the drafting process. Writers can brainstorm by freewriting, making lists, creating mind maps, or conducting research. Outlining involves organizing ideas into a structured framework, such as an outline or a concept map, to plan the structure and flow of the essay before writing the first draft.

23. Writers can use transitions to signal shifts between different ideas or sections within an essay by using transitional words and phrases, such as "however," "in addition," "furthermore," "therefore," and "conversely." Transitions help guide the reader through the argument or narrative, making the writing more cohesive and logical.

24. Writers can engage the reader's interest and attention from the beginning of an essay by using a compelling hook or opening statement, posing a thought-provoking question, providing relevant background information or context, or sharing a personal anecdote or example. The introduction should grab the reader's attention and set the stage for the rest of the essay.

25. Writers can effectively integrate quotations from sources into their own writing by introducing the quotation with a signal phrase, providing context or explanation for the quotation, and integrating it smoothly into the text. It's important to cite the source properly and to follow the conventions of the chosen citation style.

26. Revising and editing for grammar, punctuation, and spelling errors is important because it helps ensure clarity, correctness, and professionalism in writing. Errors in grammar, punctuation, and spelling can detract from the credibility of the writer and distract the reader from the content of the writing.

27. A well-developed and coherent paragraph should have a clear topic sentence that states the main idea or theme, provide supporting details or evidence to develop and illustrate the main idea, and end with a concluding sentence that summarizes the paragraph and transitions to the next. The ideas within the paragraph should flow logically and cohesively, maintaining a consistent focus on the main topic or argument.

28. Writers can vary their sentence structures and lengths for stylistic effect by using a mix of short and long sentences, simple and complex constructions, and varied sentence beginnings. Varying sentence structures adds rhythm, flow, and interest to writing, preventing monotony and engaging the reader's attention.

MATHEMATICAL REASONING

Arithmetic:

1. The product of 7.6 and 5.3 is $7.6 \times 5.3 = 40.28$.
2. $34 \times 5843 \times 85 = 16{,}886{,}270$.
3. Given $x - 7 = 15$, adding 7 to both sides gives $x = 15 + 7 = 22$.
4. The least common multiple (LCM) of 6 and 8 is 24.
5. The sum of 35 and 48 is $35 + 48 = 83$.
6. If a package contains 12 cookies and you eat 3 of them, $12 - 3 = 9$ cookies are left.
7. If $1/3553$ of a number is 24, then the number is $24 \times 3553 = 85272$.
8. If a recipe requires 2 cups of flour and you want to make 3 batches, you need $2 \times 3 = 6$ cups of flour.
9. The square root of 8181 is approximately 90.45
10. 75% expressed as a decimal is 0.75

Algebra and Functions:

11. Subtract 5 from both sides, $2x = 12$, then divide by 2, $x=6$.
12. If $y = 3x + 4$ and $x = 2$, then $y = 3(2) + 4 = 6 + 4 = 10$.
13. Solve $3(x - 4) = 15$: Expand and solve, $3x - 12 = 15$, add 12 to both sides, $3x = 27$, then divide by 3, $x = 9$.
14. If $2y - 7 = 11$, then $y = 18$, and $y = 9$.
15. Solve $4x - 9 = 27$: Add 9 to both sides, $4x = 36$, then divide by 4, $x = 9$.
16. Solve $2(3x-1) = 10$: Divide both sides by 2, $3x-1=5$, then add 1 to both sides, $3x=6$, and $x=2$.
17. Simplify $2x+3(x-2)$: Expand, $2x+3x-6=5x-6$.
18. If $y=2x+5$ and $x=3$, then $y= 2(3) + 5= 6 + 5 = 11$.
19. Solve $5x+8=33$: Subtract 8 from both sides, $5x=25$, then divide by 5, $x=5$.
20. Solve $3(y+2) = 21$: Divide both sides by 3, $y+2=7$, then subtract 2 from both sides, $y=5$.

Geometry and Measurement:

21. The area of a rectangle with length 8 meters and width 5 meters is 8×5 = 40 square meters.
22. The circumference of a circle with radius 6 inches is $2\pi r$ = 2×3.14×6 ≈ 37.68 inches.
23. The volume of a rectangular prism with length 10 cm, width 4 cm, and height 3 cm is 10×4×3=120 cubic cm.
24. The triangle with side lengths 3, 4, and 5 units is a right triangle.
25. In a triangle, the sum of the interior angles is always 180 degrees. So, angle C 180−60−120=60 degrees.
26. The area of a triangle with base 6 inches and height 8 inches is 1/2×6×8=24 square inches.
27. The perimeter of a square with side length 12 meters is 4×12=48 meters.
28. The volume of a cylinder with radius 4 inches and height 10 inches is $\pi r2h$ = 3.14 × 42 × 10 = 502.4 cubic inches.
29. A quadrilateral with angles measuring 90°, 90°, 90°, and 90° is a square.
30. If the area of a circle is 64π square units, then the radius is 8 units.
31. The area of a circle with diameter 10 inches is 78.5 square inches.
32. The surface area of a rectangular prism with dimensions 6 cm, 8 cm, and 10 cm is $2lw+2lh+2wh$=2(6×8+6×10+8×10)=2(48+60+80)=376 square cm.
33. The volume of a cone with radius 5 meters and height 12 meters is 314 cubic meters.

Data Analysis, Statistics, and Probability:

34. The mean age of the group is =24.4.
35. The median of the set {2, 5, 7, 9, 10} is 7.
36. A fair six-sided die has 3 odd numbers out of 6 total outcomes. So, the probability of rolling an odd number is 3/6=1/2.
37. The probability of drawing a blue marble from the bag is 1/3.
38. The range of heights is 70 − 62 = 8 inches.
39. The mode of the set {80, 85, 90, 92, 95} is none since all the numbers occur only once.
40. The mean of the set {4, 6, 8, 10, 12} is 8.
41. The probability of getting exactly two heads when flipping a fair coin three times is 3/8.
42. The probability of drawing a blue marble from the jar is 2/5.
43. The median age of the group is 30.
44. The range of scores is 98 − 85 = 13.
45. The probability of getting a 4 on both rolls of a fair six-sided die is 1/36.
46. The percentage of people who prefer chocolate ice cream is 60%.

SCIENCE PRACTICE

Life Sciences

1. A) Cell
2. C) Mitochondria
3. A) Photosynthesis
4. D) Neuron
5. C) To exchange gases
6. B) Nucleic acids
7. B) To fight off infections
8. C) To provide support and protection
9. A) To speed up chemical reactions
10. C) To transmit signals between body parts

Physical Sciences

11. C) H2O
12. C) Helium
13. B) 7
14. B) Sodium
15. A) NaCl
16. A) Elements are made up of atoms of the same type, while compounds are made up of atoms of different types
17. A) C6H12O6
18. B) A process that converts one substance into another
19. D) Feels slippery
20. A) Matter cannot be created or destroyed in a chemical reaction
21. 21. C) Newton
22. C) Solar power
23. A) 9.8 m/s^2
24. A) Energy cannot be created or destroyed, only transformed from one form to another
25. A) Force = mass × acceleration
26. A) Speed is a scalar quantity, while velocity is a vector quantity
27. A) The total momentum of a closed system is constant if no external forces act on it
28. B) The product of force and distance

29. A) Every object in the universe attracts every other object with a force that is directly proportional to the product of their masses and inversely proportional to the square of the distance between their centers
30. A) The rate at which work is done

Earth and Space Science:

31. C) Crust
32. D) Organic
33. B) Condensation
34. A) Gravitational pull of the Moon
35. A) Troposphere
36. A) Weather refers to short-term atmospheric conditions, while climate refers to long-term patterns of weather in a specific area
37. A) The movement of water through the Earth's atmosphere, oceans, and land
38. A) The shaking of the ground caused by the movement of tectonic plates
39. A) The movement of sediment from one place to another by wind, water, or ice
40. A) The trapping of heat in the Earth's atmosphere by greenhouse gases
41. A) The variety of species in an ecosystem
42. C) Vehicle exhaust
43. A) The trapping of heat in the Earth's atmosphere by greenhouse gases
44. B) Carbon dioxide emissions
45. A) Renewable resources can be replenished over time, while nonrenewable resources cannot
46. B) Agricultural expansion
47. A) A layer of the atmosphere that absorbs ultraviolet radiation from the Sun
48. A) Development that meets the needs of the present without compromising the ability of future generations to meet their own needs
49. D) All of the above
50. C) Greenhouse gas emissions

SOCIAL STUDIES

History:

1. A) The assassination of Archduke Franz Ferdinand
2. A) End slavery in the Confederate states
3. A) Rebuild Europe after World War II
4. B) Limited the power of the monarch and introduced the concept of constitutional government
5. B) 1863
6. A) World War I
7. A) England
8. A) 1776
9. A) George Washington

10. A) Colonizing the Americas

Geography:

1. B) Nile River
2. A) Australia
3. B) Asia
4. B) Lake Victoria
5. C) Africa
6. C) Australia
7. A) Italy
8. C) Himalayas
9. A) Africa
10. A) Ottawa

Civics and Government:

1. C) Three
2. A) The President
3. A) 13th Amendment
4. B) 100
5. B) The division of powers among the executive, legislative, and judicial branches
6. A) To make laws

7. A) Supreme Court
8. C) 27
9. B) 35 years old
10. D) The power to appoint federal judges
11. C) James Madison
12. C) The right to vote in federal elections
13. D) Lifetime appointment
14. B) 10
15. C) Judicial

Economics:

1. C) Controlling the nation's money supply and interest rates
2. A) The total value of goods and services produced within a country's borders in a given period
3. B) Sales tax
4. C) Capitalism
5. B) A sustained increase in the general level of prices for goods and services
6. A) To promote free trade and resolve disputes between member countries
7. A) A recession is a short-term economic downturn, while a depression is a severe and prolonged downturn
8. B) To protect domestic industries from foreign competition
9. B) Public transportation
10. A) It increases international trade and investment

CONCLUSION

Throughout this guidebook, we've explored the various aspects of the GED test, from its structure and content to study strategies and test-taking tips. By delving into the intricacies of each subject area – Reasoning through Language Arts, Mathematical Reasoning, Science, and Social Studies – you've gained valuable insights into what to expect on exam day and how to prepare effectively.

As you prepare to take the GED test, remember that success is not just about mastering content knowledge, but also about developing critical thinking skills, problem-solving abilities, and effective study habits. Whether you're aiming to advance your education, pursue career opportunities, or achieve personal goals, obtaining your GED credential can open doors to a brighter future.

Throughout your GED journey, perseverance and dedication will be your allies. There may be challenges along the way, but with determination and the right resources, you can overcome them. Take advantage of the study materials, practice tests, and support services available to you, and don't hesitate to reach out to educators, mentors, or fellow test-takers for guidance and encouragement.

As you approach exam day, remember to manage your time wisely, stay calm under pressure, and trust in your abilities. Trust in the preparation you've done and believe in your capacity to succeed. Keep a positive mindset, focus on the task at hand, and tackle each question with confidence.

After completing the GED test, take pride in your accomplishments, regardless of the outcome. Whether you pass with flying colors or face setbacks along the way, know that every step forward is a testament to your resilience and determination. If you don't achieve your desired score on the first attempt, don't be discouraged. Use it as an opportunity to identify areas for improvement, refine your study strategies, and come back stronger for your next attempt.

As you receive your GED credential and take the next steps towards your goals, remember that education is a lifelong journey. Embrace opportunities for continuous learning and personal growth, and never stop striving to reach new heights. Your GED credential is not just a piece of paper – it's a symbol of your hard work, determination, and commitment to excellence.

Finally, congratulations on taking the first step towards a brighter future by pursuing your GED credential. As you embark on this journey, remember that the path may be challenging, but the rewards are immeasurable. Stay focused, stay motivated, and never lose sight of your dreams. With dedication and perseverance, you can achieve anything you set your mind to. Best of luck on your GED journey – the world is waiting for you to shine!

APPENDIX

GLOSSARY OF GED TEST TERMS

GED (General Educational Development): GED refers to a set of standardized tests designed to assess and certify high school equivalency skills. It provides individuals who have not completed high school with an opportunity to earn a credential that is recognized as equivalent to a high school diploma. The GED test covers various academic subjects, including Language Arts (Reading and Writing), Mathematical Reasoning, Science, and Social Studies. Successful completion of the GED test demonstrates proficiency in these subject areas, paving the way for higher education and career opportunities.

Test-taker: A test-taker is an individual who takes the GED test. These individuals come from diverse backgrounds and may include adults seeking to further their education or improve their career prospects. Test-takers undergo preparation and study to ensure they are adequately prepared to demonstrate their knowledge and skills on the GED test.

Passing Score: The passing score is the minimum score required for a test-taker to pass each section of the GED test. Achieving the passing score indicates that the test-taker has demonstrated the necessary level of proficiency in the subject area covered by that section. The passing score may vary depending on the specific section of the GED test and is set to ensure that individuals possess the essential knowledge and skills for high school equivalency.

Section: In the context of the GED test, a section refers to a distinct part of the exam that focuses on a specific subject area. The GED test is divided into several sections, each covering different academic subjects such as Language Arts (Reading and Writing), Mathematical Reasoning, Science, and Social Studies. Test-takers must complete all sections of the GED test to earn their credential.

Passing Standard: The passing standard represents the level of proficiency or competency required for a test-taker to pass the GED test as a whole. It encompasses the passing scores for each individual section of the exam. The passing standard is established to ensure that individuals who earn a GED credential have demonstrated a sufficient level of academic knowledge and skills equivalent to that of a high school graduate.

Extended Response: An extended response is a type of question found in the Language Arts (Writing) section of the GED test. It requires test-takers to provide a written response to a prompt or question, typically in the form of an essay. Extended responses must meet specific criteria, including a minimum word count, to demonstrate the test-taker's ability to articulate their thoughts clearly and coherently.

Multiple Choice: Multiple choice is a common question format used in the GED test and other standardized assessments. In multiple-choice questions, test-takers are presented with a question or statement followed by several options or answer choices. The test-taker must select the correct answer from among the provided options.

Fill-in-the-Blank: Fill-in-the-blank is a question format in which test-takers are required to provide their own answer to complete a sentence or statement. These questions may require test-takers to recall specific information or demonstrate their understanding of concepts covered in the GED test.

True/False: True/false questions present test-takers with statements or assertions that they must evaluate as either true or false. Test-takers must carefully consider the accuracy of each statement based on their knowledge of the subject matter covered by the GED test. These questions assess the test-taker's ability to distinguish between factual information and misinformation.

GED Testing Service: The GED Testing Service is the organization responsible for developing, administering, and scoring the GED test. It oversees all aspects of the testing process, including test development, test administration, and the issuance of GED credentials. The GED Testing Service strives to ensure the integrity, fairness, and validity of the GED test to accurately assess the knowledge and skills of test-takers.

GED Credential: A GED credential is an official document awarded to individuals who successfully pass the GED test. It serves as proof of high school equivalency and is recognized by educational institutions, employers, and government agencies as equivalent to a traditional high school diploma. The GED credential opens doors to various educational and career opportunities for individuals who have not completed high school.

GED Transcript: A GED transcript is a comprehensive record of a test-taker's GED scores and credentials. It provides detailed information about the test-taker's performance on each section of the GED test, including the scores achieved and the date of completion. GED transcripts are often requested by educational institutions, employers, and other organizations as part of the application process or to verify a test-taker's academic credentials.

GED Prep: GED prep refers to the process of preparing for the GED test through study, practice, and review of relevant materials. GED prep may involve using GED preparation materials, such as textbooks, study guides, and online resources, to refresh and reinforce academic knowledge and skills. Additionally, GED prep may include enrolling in GED preparation courses or programs designed to help test-takers develop effective study strategies and improve their performance on the GED test.

GED Practice Test: A GED practice test is a simulation of the actual GED test used for preparation and assessment purposes. GED practice tests allow test-takers to familiarize themselves with the format and content of the GED test, identify areas of strength and weakness, and gauge their readiness for the official exam. GED practice tests are available in various formats, including online practice tests, printed practice booklets, and computerized testing platforms.

GED Test Center: A GED test center is a physical location where the GED test is administered to test-takers. Test centers are equipped with the necessary facilities and resources to facilitate a secure and efficient testing environment. Test-takers must schedule an appointment to take the GED test at a designated test center and adhere to the test center's policies and procedures during the testing process.

Accommodations: Accommodations are special arrangements or adjustments provided to test-takers with disabilities or special needs to ensure equal access to the GED test. Accommodations may include extended testing time, use of assistive technology, or modifications to the testing environment. The GED Testing Service offers accommodations to eligible test-takers in accordance with the Americans with Disabilities Act (ADA) and other applicable laws and regulations.

GED Ready: GED Ready is a practice test offered by the GED Testing Service to assess a test-taker's readiness for the official GED test. GED Ready practice tests are designed to closely resemble the format and content of the actual GED test, providing test-takers with an accurate assessment of their preparedness. GED Ready practice tests can help test-takers identify areas for improvement and develop a targeted study plan to enhance their performance on the GED test.

GED Test Score: A GED test score is the numerical result indicating a test-taker's performance on each section of the GED test. Test scores are based on the number of correct responses and may range from 100 to 200 for each section of the exam. GED test scores are used to determine whether a test-taker has met the passing standard and is eligible to receive a GED credential.

GED Certificate: A GED certificate is an official document awarded to individuals who pass the GED test, indicating high school equivalency. The GED certificate serves as proof that the test-taker has successfully demonstrated the knowledge and skills required for high school equivalency and is recognized by educational institutions, employers, and government agencies as equivalent to a traditional high school diploma.

GED Diploma: A GED diploma is an alternative term for the GED certificate, indicating high school equivalency. The GED diploma serves the same purpose as the GED certificate, certifying that the test-taker has successfully passed the GED test and attained high school equivalency. The GED diploma opens doors to various educational and career opportunities for individuals who have not completed high school.

Made in the USA
Las Vegas, NV
07 December 2024

13490603R00105